The Craftsman's Art Seri

CW01632479

The Craft of Gardening

Geoffrey Smith

Stanley Paul, London

Contents

Stanley Paul & Co Ltd
3 Fitzroy Square, London W1

An imprint of the Hutchinson Publishing Group

London Melbourne Sydney Auckland
Wellington Johannesburg and agencies
throughout the world

First published 1977

Set in Monotype Times

Printed in Great Britain by litho at
The Anchor Press Ltd and bound by
Wm Brendon & Son Ltd, both of
Tiptree, Essex

ISBN 0 09 128920 3 (cased)
0 09 128921 1 (paperback)

Introduction

This book explains the basics of gardening in a simple, direct and non-technical way. It assumes very little previous knowledge and it also assumes that you probably have limited space, limited time and limited money for gardening. If you work your way through it carefully you should end up:

knowing the basics of designing, planning and preparing your garden (whether it is a neglected existing plot or a brand-new one);

capable of testing your soil and knowing how to take corrective action if necessary;

knowing how to prepare and plant lawns, borders, fruit beds and vegetables;

able to carry out simple, cheap and reliable methods of plant propagation.

Gardening is a creative, money-saving and enjoyable hobby if you set about it the right way. This book attempts to show what the elements of the right way are.

1. Planning a Garden

Planning a garden layout on a plot of land recently vacated by the builders can be difficult. Equally, restoring a garden which has suffered from years of neglect also presents problems. In each instance the potential is there for creating a garden which will, over the years, provide endless pleasure and creative satisfaction.

First the site must be cleared of unwanted debris. Around a new house this will largely consist of builder's discarded material, some of which may come in useful. Sound bricks or stone can be put on one side to build frames, a patio, walls or compost bins. The broken stone or bricks will make a solid foundation for a path or garden shed. Inevitably there will be an accumulation of useless rubbish. This may be taken to a Council owned tip if transport is available. Failing this it is often worthwhile to arrange with neighbouring house owners to hire a metal skip from a waste disposal firm. It is surprising how much rubbish can be packed into a standard skip in the course of a weekend by half a dozen amateur navvies.

The neglected garden cannot be treated in quite such a wholesale manner. However, useless material such as tin cans, rusty corrugated iron, anything which cannot be burned or turned into compost can be disposed of. In addition to all the man-made litter a neglected garden also contains a tangle of unwanted vegetation. Take care not to destroy anything which might be used as the basis for a new design. Only make a minimum clearance in the first year. Remove the weeds, plus any dead or diseased garden plants. During the course of the year it will be possible to identify the various plants as they leaf or flower. Groups of bulbs should be marked so that they are not dug up during construction work. Where possible shrubs should be identified so that at the appropriate season they can be pruned back into shape. Where there is a lot of plant debris which can be rotted down it is sound policy to make a compost heap. Manures and fertilizers are becoming very expensive – compost costs nothing but the effort of making it.

Before you undertake any serious work you will need certain basic tools. A *spade* is essential for digging, levelling, planting and mixing compost. With care it will last a lifetime. Choose a blade size which will not overtax the strength of the person using it. A *rake* will make clearing up stones or weeds and seed bed preparation very much easier. A border *fork* will be a help in clearing the land of perennial weeds. Soil can be filtered through the tines of a fork to leave weed roots, couch and convolvulus exposed. A fork is also useful in breaking down rough dug land prior to raking down. A 2-gallon (10-litre) *watercan* with a special fitting for weedkiller application will be necessary if the land is heavily infested with perennial weeds. Completely eradicating convolvulus, nightshade or similar brittle-rooted weeds by digging is a laborious, time-consuming business when every tiny piece of root left in the soil grows into a new plant. One thorough application of a complete weedkiller in autumn saves hours of work and leaves the land clear for spring planting.

A pair of good quality *secateurs* and a *pruning saw* are additional items if there are overgrown trees and shrubs to be dealt with. A *garden line, wheelbarrow* and small *trowel* can be bought as required.

A new site

Certain problems occur frequently in a new garden. The builder may have skimmed the topsoil to level the foundations for house building. This topsoil should have been replaced. If it has not, then sufficient soil must be imported to cover the garden area to a depth of at least 6 inches (15 cm). Before replacing topsoil, dig over or cultivate the subsoil and leave it exposed to weather for a few weeks. This will improve the drainage and give the plants a deeper root run. Any levelling needed can be done at the same time – the area set aside for a lawn is an example. A steeply-sloping garden could be terraced with retaining walls to hold the soil. Flights of steps could connect the terraces, graded to give easy access. All this work can be completed before importing the topsoil.

Sometimes the fertile topsoil is buried under a covering of subsoil which is of poorer quality. Providing this covering is not too deep the positions can be reversed, simply by double digging the whole area. Take out a trench to the depth of the original fertile topsoil (see diagram) and 20 inches (50 cm) wide. Skim the subsoil into this, then invert the good soil on top of it. Hard work, but if a little manure, peat or compost is incorporated into the soil at the same time it produces a well-drained fertile garden.

Topsoil is the term used to describe the upper layer of soil. This is usually about 10 inches (25 cm) or the length of a spade blade deep. Subsoil for garden purpose is anything which is below that. The texture varies from the stickiest yellow, blue or grey clay, which is impossible to work with or grow anything in, to pure sand. Subsoil contains very little plant food and takes years of cultivation to convert into topsoil.

The neglected plot

The neglected plot is harder than a new site to restore but there is one considerable advantage in that there are often shrubs, even trees which can be salvaged. These give an air of maturity which a new garden takes years to achieve.

Weeds must be cleared. They make the area round the house look untidy and they compete with crop plants for food, light and space. Weedkillers can be broadly classified as selective and total, or non-selective. Selective controls applied in the right way kill only weeds. They are invaluable in freeing lawns of broad-leaved weeds while leaving the grass unharmed. They act through the foliage. Total weedkillers kill all the plants they touch through either the roots, stems or leaves. These are used almost entirely for land clearance where there are no plants of value growing.

There are complete weedkillers based on 'Paraquat' which kill only through green leaves or stems destroying only what they touch. The chemical is rendered harmless immediately it reaches the soil; these weedkillers can be used for weed control amongst established shrubs. Providing the chemical falls only on the weeds, the shrubs will be unharmed.

There are long-lasting non-selective weed controls which after one application will keep drives, paths, patios etc weed-free for twelve months. In the garden their use should be limited to these areas.

For a complete, though temporary, weed control on land to be cultivated then planted, sodium chlorate or Aminiotriazole may be applied to the soil in autumn. All poisonous chemicals should have disappeared by April the following year.

Weedkillers do not improve fertility or cultivate the soil. They do cost money but save time. Store them carefully in a cool place well away from children and pets.

By digging the soil over, hand-picking the persistent weeds and burying the remainder in the soil at least 10 inches (25 cm) deep, cultivation and weed control are performed in a single operation.

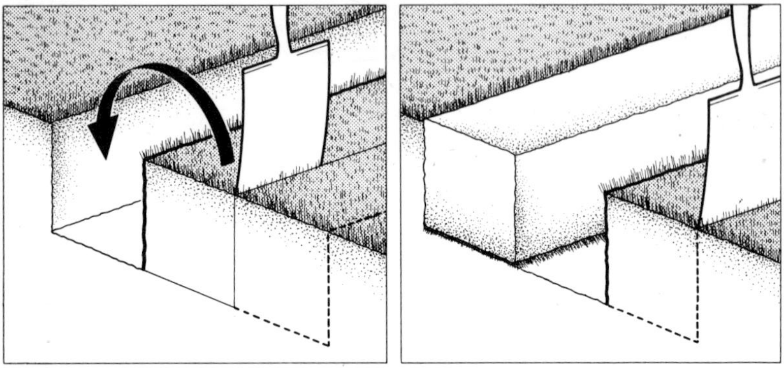

Single trenching

This turns the soil over 10–12 inches (25–30 cm) deep and is perfectly adequate for soils which are well drained. Take out a trench 10–15 inches (25–40 cm) wide; skim the weeds with the spade from the next strip of soil to be dug over and turn them upside down into the trench bottom. Dig the skimmed area over in the usual manner to fill the trench. Repeat the process until the whole plot is cultivated.

When a plot has been neglected for several years there will be a lot of dormant weed seeds which germinate each time the soil is disturbed. Providing these are removed before they can seed there will be little further trouble.

Double trenching

Double trenching turns the soil to twice the depth but without changing the position of the topsoil and subsoil. Take out a trench 20 inches (50 cm) wide and 10–12 inches (25–30 cm) deep; keep this soil to one side as it will be needed to fill in the final trench when the whole area has been turned over. Break up the bottom of the trench with a fork to a depth of a further 10 inches (25 cm). Any weeds from the next area to be dug are skimmed as in single trenching. Dig the skimmed area, inverting it to cover the weeds and fill the trench. Repeat until the whole plot has been turned over, using the soil from the first trench to fill in the last. This type of digging is useful where the subsoil is hard enough to prevent water drainage. Clay subsoils are best double dug.

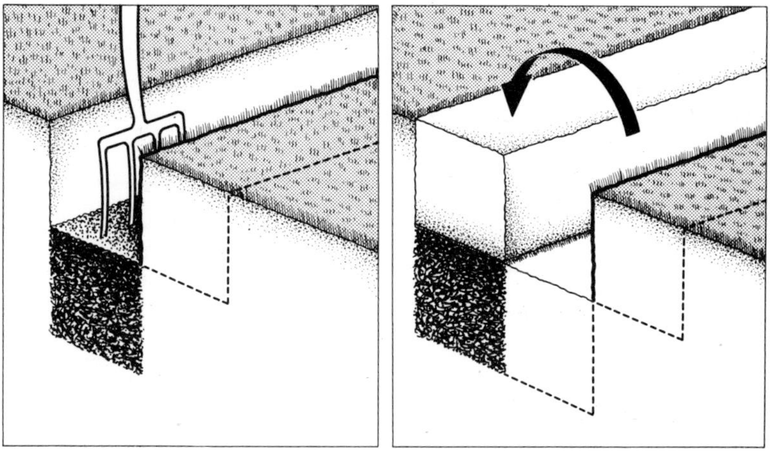

Cleaning crops

There are gardens where a so-called cleaning crop will eliminate the weeds, improve the fertility and provide vegetables for use in the home. Potatoes, Brussels sprouts and cabbage are cleaning crops. Grown in rows the push hoe can be worked between them to discourage weed growth until the heavy foliage develops enough to smother weeds.

2. Soils and How to get the best from them

Soils can vary enormously in texture, physical and chemical character. Those which contain a larger than average proportion of clay are referred to in garden terms as 'heavy'. These are difficult to work, hold a high proportion of moisture, and in many cases bake hard when dry instead of crumbling. By opening up the subsoil or raising the general level of the garden above that of the surrounding area surplus water drains away much more quickly. This is important where crops such as vegetables are to be sown direct into the open ground in spring. Wet soils are so cold that the seeds will not germinate. Only in extreme cases is it necessary to lay a complete drainage system of clay pipes to a ditch or soak-away. If you work in coarse sand or stone chips, the close texture of the clay will be broken enough to let water pass through more readily. Do the digging in early winter; then leave the surface rough for the frost to break it down to a fine crumbly surface. Heavy dressings of organic matter will increase the workability of a heavy soil, and will improve drainage and fertility. Organic matter is any material which will rot in the soil without producing any substance harmful to the plants. Farm manure, peat, compost, paper, even worn-out wool or cotton clothes can be classified as organic matter and dug into the garden.

Alkaline and acid soils

Lime is an important plant food and has a beneficial effect on soil texture particularly clay. A soil which naturally contains a lot of free lime does not need any more. The gardener needs to know if his soil contains lime for two reasons. First to know when the soil requires a lime dressing, especially important when growing vegetables as it improves the workability of the soil, releases locked-up plant foods and controls some diseases. Second, in the flower garden it is important to know if the soil contains lime because some plants such as heathers die in an alkaline soil.

A very simple method of finding out whether a soil contains lime (is alkaline) or needs lime (is acid) is to do a chemical test. A little soil taken from 4 inches (10 cm) below the surface is placed in a test tube, then shaken up with a chemical indicator which can be purchased cheaply from horticultural suppliers. Shaken up with the soil, the chemical changes colour according to the amount of lime present. This is compared against a numbered colour chart supplied with the chemical – the readings are given as numbers on a chemical scale called 'pH'. If the soil colour is equivalent to pH 7 on the scale then it is termed neutral. Any reading below that indicates a comparatively lime-free or acid condition, and a pH above 7 indicates that lime is present and the soil is termed alkaline. A pH test does *not* tell the gardener how much lime to apply, just that the soil needs or does not need a dressing.

Acidity may be neutralized by a dressing of lime or chalk, usually applied in the form of calcium carbonate, calcium hydroxide or chalk. Very acid clays will need heavy dressings of lime, 12–16 oz. per square yard (400–500 g per square metre) every three years, to ensure that crops grown in them will stay healthy.

An excess of lime in a soil can lock up essential plant foods – iron and magnesium are common examples. A shortage of either shows in susceptible plants as a yellowing of the foliage. By using plenty of farm manure or acid peat it is possible to get rid of or neutralize some of the excess lime.

At the other extreme from clay are the sandy or light soils. These drain very quickly, can be worked at almost any time and warm up early in the spring. However, plants grown in them are soon short of water in dry weather. They need regular heavy dressings of organic material to improve both water-holding and fertility. Acid sands will need dressings of lime every two years, as their free drainage soon washes out the lime.

Medium loams bridge the gap between sand and clay soils. A good deep medium loam with a pH of 6.8 is the ideal soil. It is quick to warm in spring, free-draining yet moisture-retentive. If it is properly cultivated, it will grow the full range of plants from vegetables to forest trees. Like the sand and clays it will need regular dressings of manure or compost to keep up the fertility. *All* soils are improved by dressings of organic material providing they are not waterlogged.

Supplimentary feeding of plants is occasionally necessary. A side dressing of nitrogen boosts the growth of cabbage in the spring, a regular feed helps the lawn or roses which make a lot of growth each year and exhaust the soil in which they are growing. Applying fertilizer little and often during the growing season is a good rule – but only if the plant needs it. The expense will be offset by an increased crop.

Nitrogen

Nitrogen fertilizer stimulates growth and deepens the green colouring of the leaves. Unfortunately, it dissolves so readily in water that it is soon washed out of the soil. Small applications at regular intervals save unnecessary wastage.

Phosphate

Phosphate is another essential food as it promotes healthy root growth. Bone meal, basic slag, and superphosphate of lime are three phosphate fertilizers suitable for garden use.

Potash

The third essential major plant food is potash for correcting over-luxuriant growth and stimulating flower and fruit production.

A supply of potash also gives flowers and fruit a better colour. Wood ash, sea weed, and sulphate of potash are three ways in which potash can be applied to plants.

These three – nitrogen, phosphate, and potash – are the major foods required in fairly large quantities by most plants. Minor or 'trace' elements like magnesium, manganese, iron and sulphur are usually present in sufficient quantities in a well manured or composted soil to keep the plants supplied.

Compost

Compost is a useful, economical way of improving the fertility of the soil. All the weeds, leaves of cauliflowers, broccoli, pea and bean haulms, lawn mowings, straw, in fact anything which will rot down fairly quickly can be composted. Avoid hard woody rose prunings, cabbage stalks, diseased material or perennial weeds as these are not killed by the composting process unless the heap is very well made.

Build the heap methodically as the ingredients are available, with a layer of vegetable waste followed by a sprinkle of nitrogen fertilizer or proprietary compost maker. Repeat until the heap is almost 4 feet (1.20 m) high. Dry material should be given a soaking with water. In fact, it is good policy to give the whole heap a soaking with water once a week in dry weather. A 1 inch (2½ cm) covering of soil over the heap conserves moisture and keeps the heat manufactured during the rotting process from escaping. The three essentials for producing well-made compost are moisture, warmth and air.

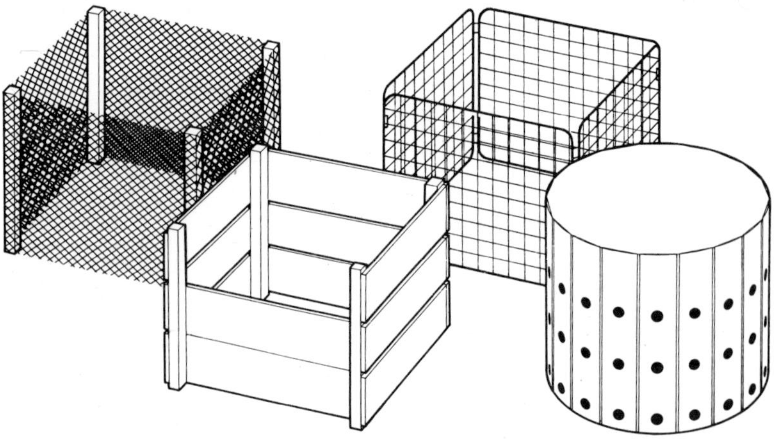

Special bins made from wooden rails spaced 1 inch ($2\frac{1}{2}$ cm) apart, or plastic covered netting keep the compost in a neat tidy heap. Two containers 4 feet (1.20 m) by 4 feet by 4 feet high will hold all the waste material an average-sized household needs to dispose of. Bins may be bought ready-made in a wide variety of shapes and sizes.

3. Siting of Permanent Features

The new garden will be without any amenities. Possibly the builder will have laid a path, but there is unlikely to be a shed, a greenhouse or frames.

The siting of the paths and other facilities is important because of their bearing on the working of the garden and its design. Structural items, like greenhouses, paths, a pool or rock garden, once in position are laborious to move so give them a great deal of thought before doing any building. Possibly the demands of a young family mean provision must be made for a sand pit, Wendy house or swing. To be of any real use these must be given a sunny position. As the children grow out of playing in sand pits the area can be made into a garden for them to cultivate.

Simple planning and paths

Plan the paths first. They give access to the garden in all weathers and enable materials to be moved easily from place to place. Keep the path to one side of the plot rather than across the centre. Central paths restrict ball games and make any sort of spacious design impossible. Paths should be made of materials that are durable, easy to maintain and safe to walk on. There are five main types of garden paving. On-site concreting, where wet concrete is levelled between a framework of boards, is probably the easiest to construct and maintain but never seems to blend into the landscape. I recommend instead:

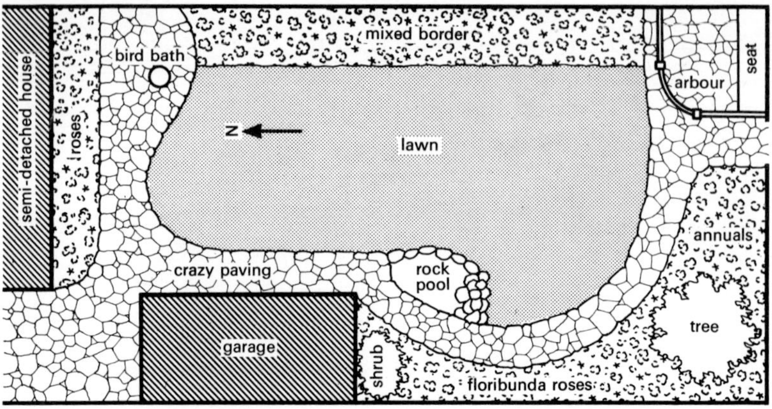

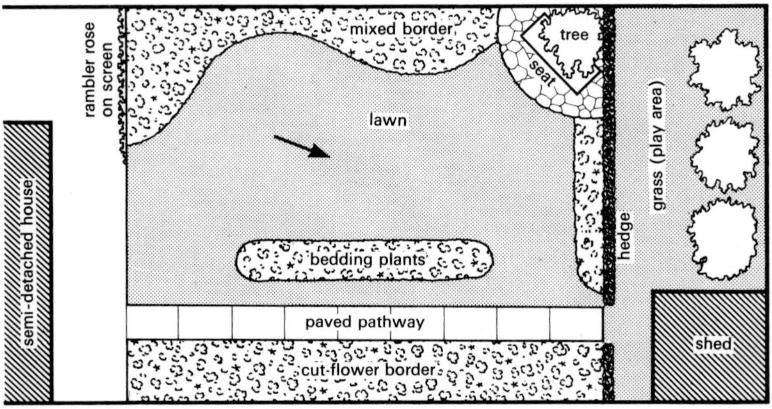

Slab paving: Slabs of manufactured or natural stone are laid on a mortar or sand bed.

Brick paving: This is not common because of the labour required, but it will form a most attractive, durable path. Only the hardest bricks – 'stocks' or 'wirecuts' should be used, laid on a 2–3 inch (5–7 cm) concrete base. Various patterns can be drawn with the bricks to give additional interest.

Tiles: They are so expensive now that few people can afford them. Where cheap demolition 'seconds' are available it is worth considering them for small areas. For stability they must be laid on a concrete base.

Gravel: Paths of gravel, stone chippings and similar materials, unless bonded with a fixative – concrete, bitumen or similar adhesive – tend to lift in frosty weather and stick to muddy shoes.

Greenhouses

Before actually choosing and buying a greenhouse it is advisable to check with the local planning and rating authorities about bye-laws. A greenhouse attached to the house could mean a rate increase. Even worse a large greenhouse erected without planning permission could mean an order to remove the structure, so check first.

A tenant should remember that a greenhouse or shed erected on a permanent concrete or brick base becomes a landlord's fixture. Though a solid brick or concrete base ensures stability and preserves the life of a structure the tenant householder may be well advised to consider alternative bases: a breeze-block dolly, or wood or metal base plates.

Greenhouses vary in shape which makes choosing a design tailor-made to suit the site so much easier. *Span* houses have both sides of the roof equal in length. *Threequarter span* houses have a roof nearer the ground on one side than the other. *Lean-to* houses are built against a wall; these are easier to heat but, of course, admit less light and are difficult to ventilate. The modern *circular* or *hexagonal* greenhouse is worth considering where space is limited, and can become a focal point of the design.

Greenhouses may be glazed right to soil level, so the crops can be planted direct into beds on the greenhouse floor. The alternative is to have vertical walls made of wood, concrete, brick or metal

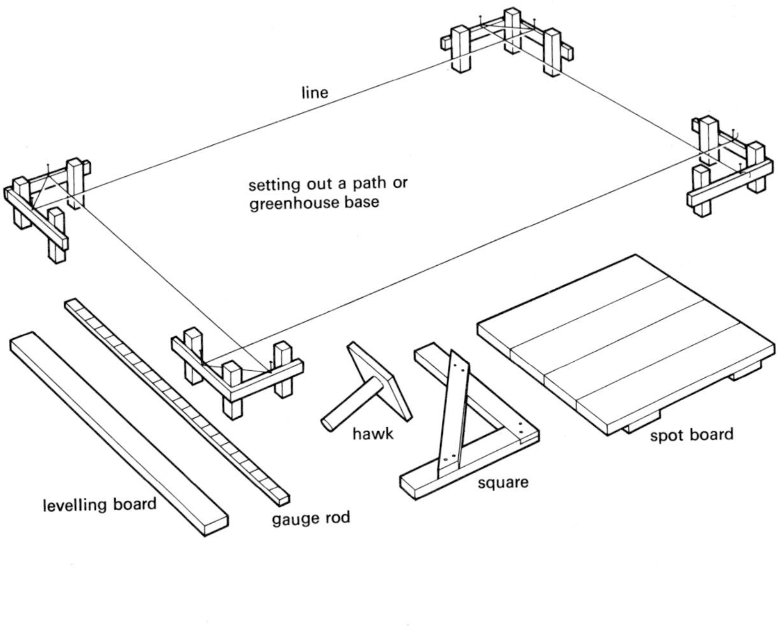

with the greenhouse resting on these, and plants in pots on a staging. This method of construction gives better heat retention than glass to ground houses.

Greenhouses are built of wood or aluminium alloy. The soft woods (which until recently were predominantly used) needed regular painting if they were to last any length of time. Western red cedar is the most widely used of all woods in amateur greenhouse construction. Treating cedar with a preservative every two years is much less time-consuming than the painting required for other soft woods. Aluminium alloys need little maintenance and are becoming increasingly popular. Polythene structures are at present a short-term alternative to the normal glass.

Choose a sheltered place for erecting the house. Too much wind breaks the glass and also causes excessive heat loss. Easy access is also important – a greenhouse situated near the house tends to be given more attention than one at the far end of the garden. Avoid a position which is in shade for the greater part of the day: plants need all the light available, particularly in winter.

Whether the long side of the greenhouse runs north–south or east–west is largely governed by the space available. There are advantages to each alignment: east–west gives one shady and one sunny side with better winter light, north–south gives a more even light distribution all the year round.

Electrical heating with a thermostat-controlled unit is a clean, efficient, trouble-free means of maintaining an even temperature. All electrical heating is expensive and the cost increases dramatically with every lift in the greenhouse temperature. Lining the greenhouse with polythene conserves heat and cuts fuel bills whatever form of heating is used. The polythene is put on in early November and removed in April. The most economical way of using electricity in the garden is by installing soil warming cables, buried in the greenhouse border or in sand or soil on a staging. This form of heating keeps the roots of the plants warm and reduces appreciably the amount of heat required.

Natural gas is a non-poisonous fuel now being used for greenhouse heaters and where available provides an alternative choice to electricity.

The oil-fired boiler controlled by a thermostat is efficient. Installation charges are high and running costs have trebled over the last two years but as with electricity and gas there are few maintenance worries. The heaters are efficient and can be left for long periods without attention.

The paraffin stove is the most popular form of emergency heating for the amateur but to be efficient needs regular attention – wick-trimming and filling. They do not switch off automatically when the temperature rises which can be very wasteful. Intelligently used they function reasonably well.

Solid fuel heaters are constantly being improved but unlike electric, gas and oil heaters need daily attention – stoking and cleaning. An electrically operated thermostat can be fitted to prevent wastage of fuel.

When choosing a heater several factors must be taken into consideration:

1. Purchasing price and installation costs: is this offset by the efficiency of the unit?
2. Running cost: fuel prices are constantly changing – always upwards.
3. The amount of time which can be devoted to looking after the unit.

Your greenhouse will need a water supply, either piped or rain-water. If the local piped supply contains lime it is essential to

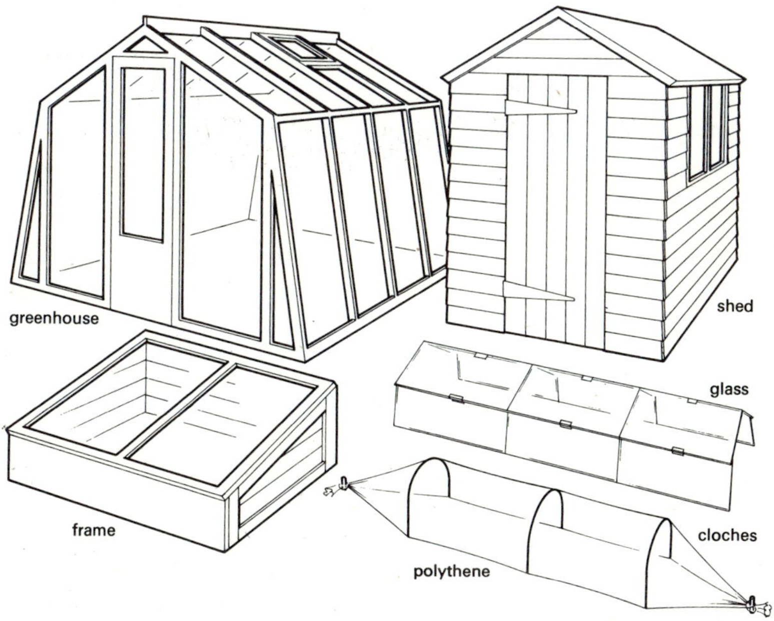

conserve rainwater for plants such as heathers and rhododendrons which do not like lime.

Frames

Sometimes a greenhouse cannot be accommodated in the garden so a frame could be used as a substitute. A large frame with soil-warming can be used to raise flowers and vegetables from seed. During the winter it serves to protect pot plants.

A very serviceable frame can be built from wood, bricks, breeze-blocks or cement. The covering made from glass or polythene should be light enough to be easily removed. There are several metal frames available which have glazed sides, easily adjusted ventilation and need scarcely any maintenance, painting, etc.

Garden sheds

You are bound to need a garden shed for storing tools, compost and fertilizer unless your house is well supplied with out-buildings. The shed is most conveniently situated near the greenhouse. The various aspects provided by the shed walls may be used for growing climbing plants. Choose a shed sufficiently large to accommodate all the tools needed for the garden with space to spare for a bench. The bench may be portable so it can be used outside for seed sowing, potting and other garden work when the weather is suitable. A good solid second-hand table can often be bought for less money than the materials to build a bench, so is an alternative worth exploring.

Ornamental versus edible

Only you can decide how much space is allocated to growing food crops and how much to flowers. With the increasing cost of fruit and vegetables many want to devote a major portion at least of their back gardens to vegetables. If in due course there is over-production then the area can be reduced. On the other hand, once a border is filled with expensive shrubs you may feel reluctant to throw them all away to make room for vegetables.

Shelter is vitally important in most forms of gardening, particularly with vegetable growing.

The greatest economies are made if the home-grown crops are available when the same articles in the shops are expensive.

Ornamental, internal hedges are an expensive luxury in a small vegetable plot. A barrier of gooseberry or blackcurrant bushes provides the same shelter as an ornamental hedge and a crop of fruit as well. Modern high-density building and the reduced garden area means utilizing every inch of space in this way.

Buy two-year old bushes, plant them 3 feet (1 m) apart and allow them to run together to form an effective barrier.

Hedges

In the ornamental garden the hedge must provide shelter and make a contribution to the overall landscape. A good hedge should be easy to grow on most types of soil. It must need the minimum of maintenance while affording the maximum shelter. Two further requirements rather harder to meet: the chosen plants should be cheap and readily obtainable.

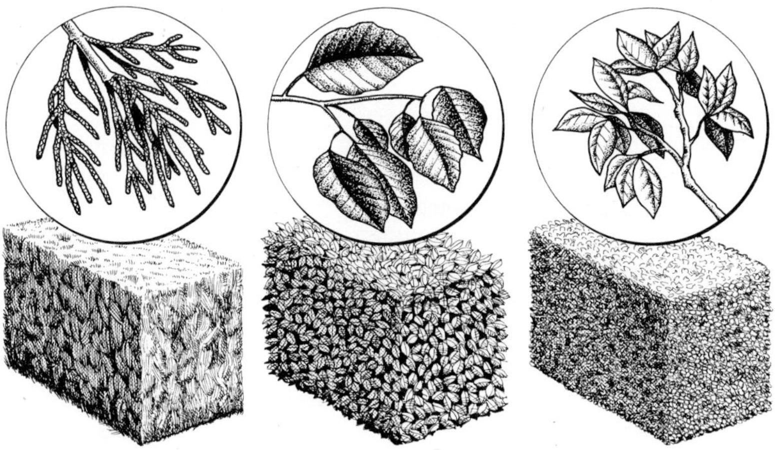

Cupressocyparis leylandii *Fagus sylvatica* *Prunus cerasifera*

X Cupressocyparis leylandii, an evergreen conifer, grows quickly, thrives in most soils and needs clipping at most twice a year – May and again in August. Plant 30 inches (75 cm) apart.

Chamaecyparis lawsoniana, 'Green Hedge', another evergreen conifer possesses all the virtues found in the cupressocyparis, but grows at half the speed. Trim once a year in either May or August. Plant 30 inches (75 cm) apart.

Fagus sylvatica, beech, though a forest tree, may be trained to make a hedge of any height from 6 to 40 feet (2 to 12 m). Any reasonably well-drained soil is suitable, and by clipping twice a year beech can be kept as a tight, almost impenetrable barrier. Plant 15 inches (35 cm) apart. In certain locations a foliage effect achieved by planting three copper and five green leaved beech can be most attractive. The leaves are retained in a dry state throughout the winter so the hedge is attractive all the year round.

Prunus cerasifera 'Pissardii'. Another foliage effect is created by planting five of the *Prunus cerasifera* 'Pissardii' which has purple leaves to three of the type plant *P. cerasifera* which has pale green. The bushes are planted 24 inches (60 cm) apart. Clipping is usually necessary twice a year.

Roses. Tall growing floribunda roses make good hedges. 'Queen Elizabeth' is an example – space 18 inches (45 cm) apart and prune in early March.

Almost all trees and shrubs which will stand hard pruning can be trained to make a formal hedge.

The site for the hedge should be dug to a depth of 18 inches (45 cm). Remove all perennial weeds and dress the soil with well rotted manure, peat or compost.

Evergreen hedges are planted in spring (March–April), deciduous (plants which loose their leaves) at any time when soil conditions are suitable during the winter months.

Where facilities are not available to plant a hedge, a wall or fence will provide the same shelter and privacy.

Walls

Whether of stone, brick or concrete, walls are expensive to erect. With a little care, a moderately practical person can build a patio, retaining or internal wall, and with the experience gained proceed to erecting a boundary wall.

Foundations of the boundary wall must be firm. For a 4½ feet (1·4 m) wall foundations 18 inches (45 cm) wide by as much deep of rammed hardcore and concrete would be required.

Fences

Fences do not have the same permanence as a wall, but if you leave them without plant covering they are not very attractive. Wooden posts should be treated with a preservative before being inserted in the ground. Use a chemical which is not harmful to plants. For

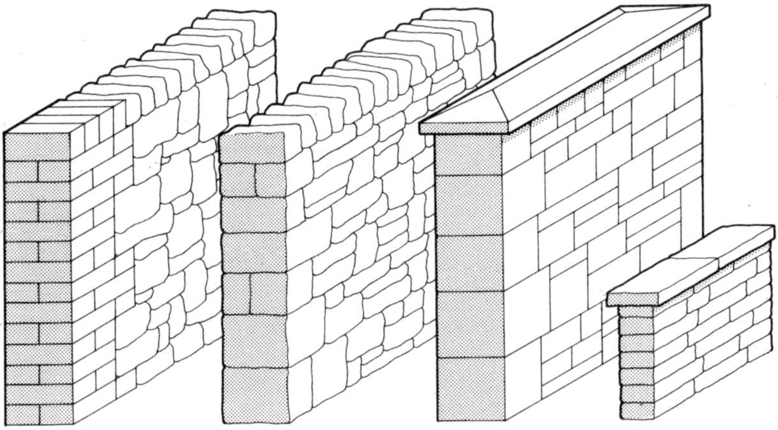

uncoursed random rubble with brick quoining | coursed random rubble | coursed square rubble | dwarf wall

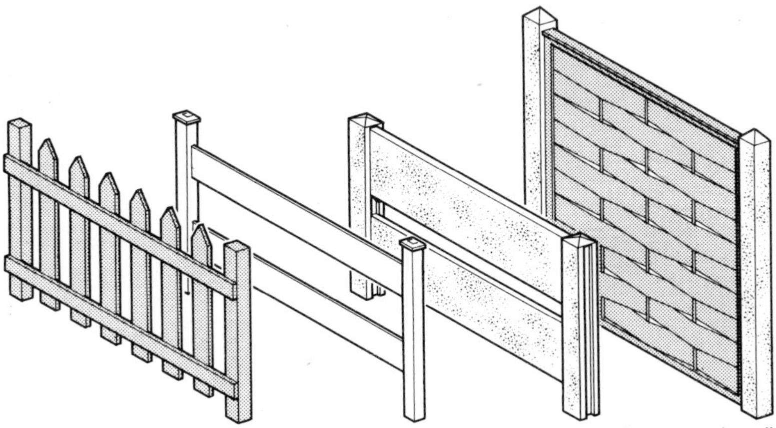

wood | PVC | concrete | interwoven (wood)

example the fumes from creosote can cause leaf scorch. When the posts will be carrying a lot of weight as with overlapping panel fencing 5 feet (1.5 m) high the supports should be bedded in a concrete socket. This lessens the risk of the fence being blown down in a strong wind.

By fixing galvanized or plastic-covered wire to the posts the fence may serve as a support to climbing plants adding beauty to the garden.

4. Individual Features

Patio and terrace gardens

A well-proportioned terrace or patio is the most convenient way of linking the house and garden together. Ideally the terrace is in full sun or only partially shaded and can be used as an outdoor room whenever conditions permit. In a small garden the whole area may be paved with plants grown on the boundary wall, fence or in containers to soften the bare expanse of stone work. Shape and size of the terrace are governed by the design of the rest of the garden rather than the house. When the garden is informal the terrace should echo this with curving or irregular lines. A rigidly formal garden design should be repeated in a square symmetrical terrace.

Where the house is raised well above the garden area the steps leading down to the lawn must be shallow, so it is easy to walk and carry things down them. Hard angles can be softened by planting low-growing shrubs so as to mask the stone work.

Leave pockets between the stonework for growing suitable plants, but be careful that these do not interfere with the usefulness of the terrace as a sitting-out area.

Conifers

Juniperus procumbens 'Nana'

Juniperus sabina 'Tamariscifolia'

Shrubs

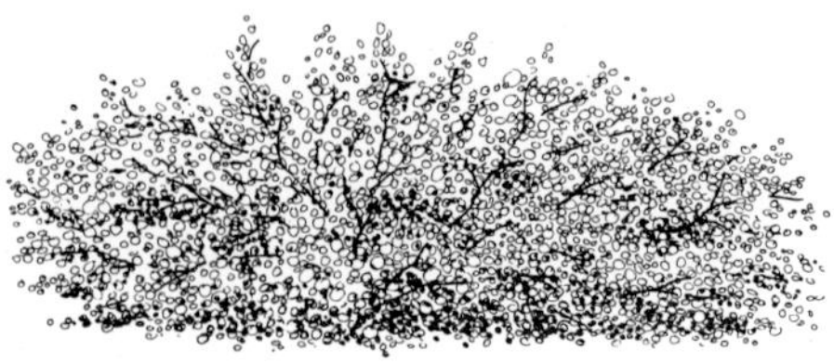

Cytisus kewensis

Potentilla fruiticosa

Prostrate shrubs for masking step edges

Conifers

Juniperus procumbens 'Nana' with grey foliage.

Juniperus sabina 'Tamariscifolia' with mid-green foliage.

Shrubs

Cytisus x kewensis grows only 12 inches (30 cm) high and has pale yellow flowers in May.

Iberis sempervirens, a hardy evergreen shrub, 9 inches (22 cm) high, bears white flowers in May and June.

Potentilla fruticosa 'Elizabeth' up to 18 inches (45 cm) high, has yellow flowers throughout the summer.

Viburnum davidii is rather taller, up to 24 inches (60 cm), and makes an evergreen mound of foliage. The white flowers which appear in June are followed by blue berries when both male and female forms are planted.

All shrubs which are sufficiently prostrate and not too vigorously spreading are suitable for masking step edges.

A small bed may be left at the junction between house and patio or terrace to accommodate climbing plants. Utilization of walls and fences is important in a small plot as it appreciably extends the space which can be gardened.

Tubs, hanging baskets and window boxes

These can be used to soften the hard line of a house. Tubs are suitable for corners of the garden which need seasonal interest, as for example the top of a low terrace wall or an entrance porch. Tubs and urns can be obtained in a wide variety of shapes and materials. Replicas in polystyrene of the old stone urns, baskets and basins so much a feature of stately homes can be obtained at a fraction of the cost of an original. They are much lighter by comparison, though once filled with soil any container is cumbersome to move.

Concrete containers, either precast or moulded on the site make durable plant holders. They are heavy and it is advisable to raise them on a wooden frame fitted with castors.

Tubs made from half beer barrels or wooden boxes treated with a

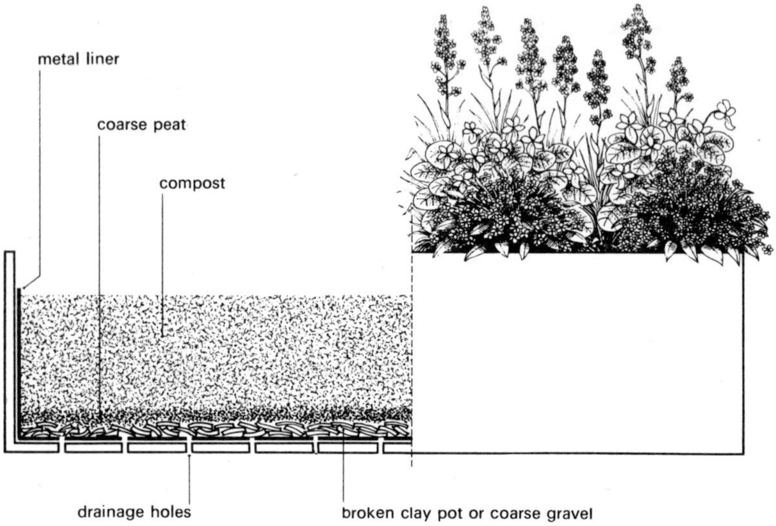

wood preservative will last many years. Wooden tubs can be made without too much difficulty to fit awkward-shaped corners by anyone handy with a hammer and saw. *Do not* treat wooden plant containers with *creosote* as the fumes can damage or kill plants.

Window boxes traditionally made in wood are frequently fitted with a removable metal liner 6–8 inches (15–20 cm) deep which extends their life considerably. They are also now being made in polystyrene.

All containers must have drainage holes in the bottom, sufficient to make sure all surplus moisture drains away.

Hanging baskets are usually only used from about mid May until late September. They are useful for covering bare house walls, decorating patios or terrace walls and entrances. Modern baskets are made of plastic covered wire. When fitting hanging baskets or window boxes make certain the supports are adequate.

Filling window boxes

The ready-made composts, based on either soil or peat, obtainable from garden shops, will suit most plants. These composts are expensive so only use them if the soil in the garden is very poor. To make your own mix 7 shovelfulls of soil from the vegetable garden with 4 shovelfulls of peat and 2 or 3 shovelfulls of coarse sand. To every barrow load of the mixture add a 5-inch (12 cm) potfull of John Innes base fertilizer or fishmeal.

Place a layer of broken clay pot of coarse gravel in the bottom of the container, and cover it with coarse peat or partially rotted leaves. This makes sure the drainage holes will function. Fill up the tubs with the compost to within 3 inches (8 cm) of the top. Most of the plants normally used for bedding out may be used to fill window boxes or tubs. In autumn plant up polyanthus, viola, wallflowers, myosotis, tulips, hyacinths, or any other suitable spring-flowering subjects. During early June these are removed, the tubs given a light dusting of peat to which fishmeal or John Innes fertilizer has been added and the summer-flowering plants installed. As well as the summer bedding, many greenhouse and house plants can spend the summer outdoors in tubs or window boxes – fuchsia, pelargoniums, ficus, campanula, sansieveria, etc.

To save labour the containers can be planted up with shrubs such as camellia, rhododendrons and skimmia for the shady places. Senecio, *Laurus noblis* (bay), hebe, roses and a wide variety of conifers for the sunnier corners.

Filling hanging baskets

Hanging baskets are first lined with sphagnum moss or plastic sheeting (black or green preferably) then filled with a good-quality, weed-free potting compost. Because the basket is seen mostly from below it is best filled with a majority of trailing plants. Ivy-leaved pelargoniums, pendulous begonia, fuchsia, trailing lobelia, nasturtiums and *campanula isophylla* are all suitable for growing in hanging baskets. Once the basket is filled cover any bare earth with sphagnum moss,

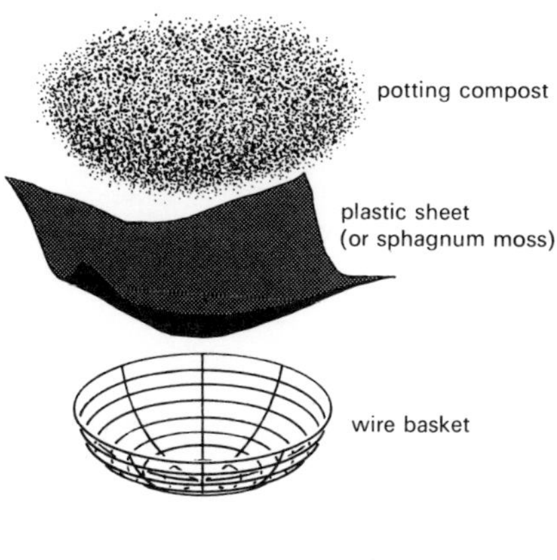

then thoroughly water and in ten to fourteen days it will be ready to go on display.

Containers dry out much more quickly than open garden plantings so you must water them regularly.

5. Lawns

First the area set aside for the lawn must be well drained and cultivated. Dig the soil over removing all perennial weeds. Any levelling must be done at this stage. For most gardens the lawn need not be bowling-green level but where the site is very uneven it is best to use pegs, levelling board and a spirit level. Remove the topsoil, grade out the subsoil, then replace the topsoil to the level of the pegs. This is hard, heavy work especially if the soil is clay. Topsoil may be available in quantity at a reasonable price in which case it is worthwhile buying enough to level the site without having to excavate the existing clay. When the soil is in poor condition the physical texture will be improved by scattering two or three shovelfulls of well-made compost, rotted manure, powdered seaweed or peat to each square yard or metre, to be raked in as the plot is levelled.

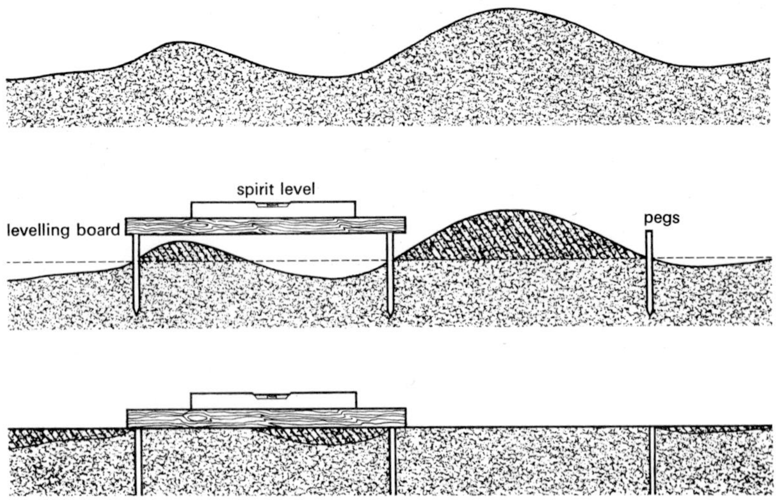

Lawns from seed

Choose a seed mixture which will suit not only the soil but also the purpose for which the lawn will be used, which may be for games, as a sitting-out area or purely ornamental. Seedsmen are happy to advise on this. In general avoid mixtures for the ornamental lawn which include rye grass. Where a hard-wearing sward is of first importance then a mixture which includes a proportion of rye grass will be most suitable. For example a bowling green mixture would be made up of 80 per cent chewings red fescue and 20 per cent New Zealand brown top bent. A hard-wearing lawn in constant use as a playground would be based on a mixture of 40 per cent Chewings red fescue, 30 per cent S 23 rye grass, 20 per cent crested dogs tail and 10 per cent rough-stalked meadow grass. In general the coarser grass mixtures are quicker growing. For areas of the lawn which are shaded use mixtures which include smooth, rough-stalked and wood meadow grass.

Firm the soil with the feet and rake it down to a fine, level seed bed. A light general fertilizer dressing can be worked in just to give the germinating seed a good start.

Sowing may be carried out whenever the weather permits from mid April onwards. Mid August to mid September is the ideal time as the soil is warm and germination takes place quickly, and the dews are heavy enough to keep the seedlings growing.

Sow the seed at $1\frac{1}{2}$ oz. per square yard (50 g per square metre). Providing the soil is well prepared and the seed has been treated with a bird repellent any more is wasteful. After sowing rake the seed lightly into the top $\frac{1}{4}$ inch ($\frac{3}{4}$ cm) of soil. Once the grass is germinated and growing it should be lightly rolled (the roller on the mower will be enough). This has the effect of making the grass spread instead of growing just a single blade. *Do not* roll at all when the soil is *wet*.

Some six to eight weeks after sowing, when the grass is 1–$1\frac{1}{2}$ inches (3–4 cm) high, whisk it with a broom to remove worm casts, then cut it with the mower blades freshly sharpened and set so as to just tip the grass. In three or four days cut again, gradually reducing the height until the lawn is being cut with the blades set $\frac{3}{4}$ inch (2 cm) high.

Turfing

Turfing is more expensive but gives the quickest results. Buy good-quality turf; just as much effort goes into laying good turf as bad and no amount of work will turn inferior turf into a good-quality lawn.

The bed is prepared in exactly the same way as for seeding: digging, removing perennial weeds, working in compost, peat, rotted manure or powdered seaweed and raking in a dressing of fertilizer as the levelling down is done.

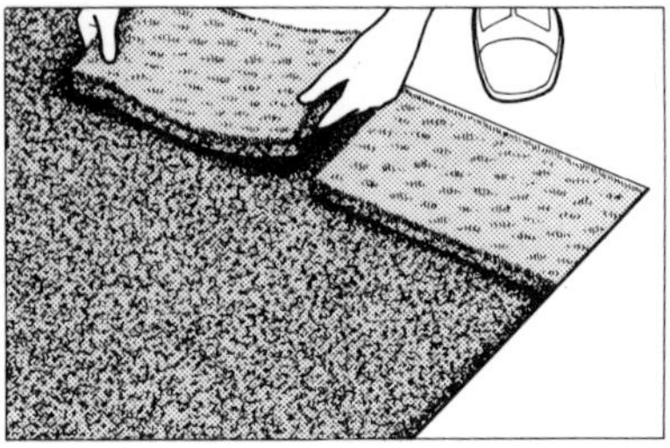

Start turfing from a corner, staggering the joints between the rows like bricks in a wall. By starting every alternate row with a half turf the joints will fall in the right place automatically. Each turf should be pushed firmly into position against the one that precedes it. Lay a plank on the first row of turves to lay the second one and so on until the lawn is completed. A large piece of heavy planking 2–3 feet (75–90 cm) long by 12–18 inches (30–45 cm) wide nailed to a wooden handle may be used to level the turf into position. Alternatively, a day or two after turfing is completed the area can be rolled once across the line and once up and down the line to help bind the turf into position.

Cutting begins when the grass obviously needs it. Turves laid in December will need no further attention until spring, whereas turf laid in May will need cutting with the blades set $1\frac{1}{2}$ inches (4 cm) high some ten to fourteen days after laying.

Keep both seeded and turfed lawns well watered in dry weather.

Routine lawn care is essential. For regular mowing set the blades approximately $\frac{3}{4}$ inch (2 cm) high. Mowing too closely leads to bare patches which are soon invaded by moss or weeds. Remove the box in dry weather so the clippings are returned as a mulch. *Do not* cut when the weather is wet as this compacts the soil.

Start feeding in April after the second or third cut, 2 oz. to the square yard (70 g per square metre) of a standard lawn fertilizer. If the lawn is weed-infested apply a selective weedkiller a week after feeding. Further fertilizer applications with increased nitrogen will maintain the grass in healthy growth – 1–2 oz. per square yard

(35–70 g per square metre) at six-week intervals. In August add extra potash and lower the nitrogen so that the growth is slowed down. Too much nitrogen late in the season means soft lush growth which is quickly attacked by fungus disease or damaged by frost.

Regular brushing and raking, especially in autumn, removes the mat of dead grass which accumulates at soil level. After the autumn raking spike the lawn. Use a hollow tined fork which removes a core of soil if the soil is heavy clay; on lighter soils an ordinary garden fork will do. Spiking breaks up the hard crust which forms on the soil due to treading and mowing, and the deep penetrating tines allow air and rainwater to get right to the grass roots.

When practicable the grass will benefit from a dressing of compost, sand mixed with sieved loam or peat or old tomato compost. Just a thin dressing brushed into the surface so as not to smother the grass.

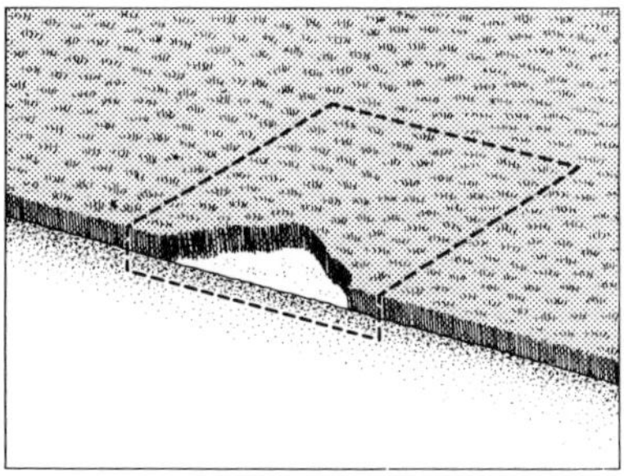

Patch worn or diseased areas when convenient, usually during the winter months. Cut out the piece to be repaired. If they are fungus-infected treat the hole with a fungicide. The patch should be slightly larger than the hole to leave room for settling. Discoloured areas on the lawn indicate fungal infection (fusarium). They should be watered with a solution of $\frac{1}{2}$ oz. of sulphate of iron to a gallon of water (3 g per litre).

Balanced feeding and regular cutting with a well-maintained lawnmower will produce a beautiful sward which becomes a focal point in the garden.

6. The Mixed Border

There is little to be gained by keeping herbaceous plants, shrubs and bulbs separate in a small garden. By considering each part of the garden design as a single unit yet part of an overall pattern, each plant you grow is shown to full advantage.

For example, this spring design is comparatively simple yet always beautiful: a weeping birch underplanted with spring bulbs, crocus, snowdrops and miniature narcissus. There is the perennial interest of the white stem and attractive shape of the birch with the spring bulbs contributing seasonal points of colour. Include some yellow-flowered pansy and autumn-blossoming *Cyclamen neapolitanum*, and the picture is complete for the twelve months.

When you have a small area to garden every inch of space must be filled. Walls and boundary fences can be planted to form a background before the line of the mixed border is filled in. Think of your garden area as on three levels. The highest is formed by the trees whose height and spread in maturity will not spoil the rest of the garden. Below these is the shrub line, and finally the bulbs, herbaceous plants and annuals which cover every bare patch of soil.

To support so many plants your soil needs to be in a well-cultivated, fertile condition. The best way to prepare the bed is to double dig it (pages 6–8).

Shrubs

These are expensive so the design of the border needs careful planning. If you have an overall plan the expense can be spread over several years, instead of trying to purchase enough plants to fill the empty space all at once. The gaps can be made up with annuals raised from seed, then as the major plan fills in these can be discarded.

You need not restrict the planting to the dormant season. By buying shrubs or perennials grown in containers you can extend the work throughout the year. This, however, costs rather more and you could spend the money saved by restricting the work to the period from October to mid April on more plants.

Choose a mild day for planting when the soil is dry enough to work on without half the garden sticking to your shoes. Take out a hole large enough to accommodate the roots when fully spread out.

Trim away any roots which are broken or bruised and replace the soil, shaking it down amongst the fine root hairs so that no air pockets are left and firm well with the feet. On heavy clay do not over-firm, leave the surface 2 inches (5 cm) loose and do not bury the roots too deep.

Tall shrubs or trees need a stake in exposed places. Put this on the side from which the prevailing wind comes so that there is no danger of the stems rubbing on the support. Secure the tree to the stake with twine or a patent tree tie. Check for damaged, dead or diseased branches. These should be cut away with a sharp pair of secateurs. Paint the wounds you make with Stockholm tar to prevent diseases infecting them.

Decide where the focal points in the border are to be. Look at the garden from the house, from both ground-floor and bedroom windows. Permanent features like trees and shrubs are installed first and the rest of the design arranged so as to compliment them. No garden is ever complete or perfect; there is always something new to be fitted into the pattern.

You will find a border easier to look after if all the plants in a group require the same routine feeding. For example, rhododendrons enjoy a cool, moist soil, so bulbs like snowdrops and bluebells fit easily into the pattern because a mulch of peat would keep them all happy.

Lilacs are best suited by a soil which is well drained and contains lime, so underplant with daffodils, then give them both a dressing of coarse bonemeal mixed with well-rotted compost each year in February.

Do not let your newly-planted border dry out. This means regular watering throughout the first summer. Spray the leaves from overhead so the leaves are moistened then the water drips down on to the roots. In exposed borders newly-planted evergreens need shelter from wind until the roots take hold. A sheet of polythene stretched tightly between three canes makes a simple but effective windbreak.

Feeding should not be necessary the first year; give the roots time to hold in the soil. In spring the following year dust the soil with a balanced fertilizer containing nitrogen, phosphates and potash at the rate of 2 oz. per square yard (70 g per square metre). A mulch of peat, rotted manure or compost will keep the soil cool, moist and in good physical condition.

Pruning

You should aim always to keep plants healthy. Each time diseased, damaged or dead wood appears cut the offending branch out as close to the main stem as possible. Do not leave unsightly stumps, and paint over any large wounds with a waterproof compound such as Stockholm tar.

Secondly, you should keep the tree in good shape by removing crossing or surplus branches. Thirdly the tree should show the beauty of flower, foliage or stem to best effect. For example, all the branches growing low enough down to spoil the white stem of a silver birch should be removed. Or an even better illustration would be *Cornus alba* 'Sibirica' whose young growths are bright scarlet. By cutting older stems back hard in April you encourage the plant to grow a mass of brightly-coloured young stems which look lovely throughout autumn and winter.

Spring-flowering shrubs such as forsythia should be pruned immediately they finish flowering, cutting out the oldest branches to make way for young vigorous shoots which will carry flowers the next year. Summer flowering shrubs like *Buddleia davidii* or philadelphus should be pruned during winter, before early February.

Overgrown evergreens – holly and broad-leaved laurel – can be cut back hard in early May. Strong young shoots will soon break from below the wound and these have time to mature before the autumn.

Herbaceous plants

Herbaceous plants are much easier to keep neat in a mixed border than if grown in a border to themselves. The taller-growing shrubs shelter them from the worst effects of strong winds. Overgrown plants can be lifted, divided and replanted with far less effort than would be required to renew a complete herbaceous border. You can lift any which are overcrowded. Divide them, discard the old woody portions and keep the young, vigorous, well-rooted healthy shoots. Before re-planting them prepare the soil by forking in a dressing of moist peat or compost and 2 oz. of balanced fertilizer to the square yard (70 g per square metre).

Plants such as delphiniums with thick fleshy roots are best propagated by taking cuttings of young growths in spring when they are 3–4 inches (7–10 cm) long. These cuttings will root if dipped in rooting powder and inserted in a mixture of two parts sand and one part peat.

Bulbs

When to plant bulbs depends on the type being grown. Narcissus (daffodils) are usually on sale from September onwards so you can buy and plant straight away. You should remember daffodils do not grow well in freshly-manured soil. Plant the bulbs 4–6 inches (10–15 cm) deep. Tulips may be bedded out in bays in a mixed border during late October to November, choosing the best-drained positions. Depth of planting varies according to size of bulb, but 2–4 inches (5–10 cm) between the top of the bulb and the soil surface is a useful guide.

You should always lift snowdrops for division and replanting just as the flowers fade – there is less chance of failure then. When they are dried, only a percentage grow.

Crocus which flower in spring should be planted up by the end of November, while those which flower in autumn should be established in their flowering positions by August at the latest. Often it is a case of planting the bulbs when they are available from specialist nurseries or in the shops.

Climbers

The following climbers will rapidly cover a fence, building, or can be trained out over a tall growing shrub.

Clematis montana 'Alexander' is a very vigorous climber which produces a billowing mass of white, sweetly scented flowers during May to early June. Excellent for covering ugly features. The pink form sold as 'Rubens' flowers just as well but lacks the fragrance.

Hedera, better known by the common name ivy, are useful in areas of dense shade or in densely-populated places with a high degree of atmospheric pollution. Forms of the Persian ivy, like *Hedera colchica* 'Dentata variegata' have large, attractively variegated cream on green leaves. More easily grown in poor soil are the forms of common ivy, so when you are in doubt choose from an enormous list of varieties whose leaf colours include dark green, cream on pale green, and gold.

Hydrangea peteolaris, the climbing hydrangea, will grow on a north wall but you get more flowers by giving it a place in the sun. As with the ivy this lovely plant climbs by means of airial roots along the undersides of the branches.

Jasminum nudiflorum, whose brilliant yellow flowers do so much to dispel the grey gloom of winter, appreciates a sunny position. Where possible, space the branches out on a wall or trellis so that pruning, which is best carried out when the plants have finished flowering in April, is easier. Groups of the early flowering *Crocus* 'Whitewell Purple' planted below the climber will seed themselves over the years to form a carpet of flowers and afford a contrast to the yellow jasmine.

Russian vine. There are times when a quick climber is the easiest and cheapest way of hiding an unsightly but necessary feature. The Russian vine – *Polygonum baldschuanicum* – will romp over a building, bare bank or tree with complete impartiality. By planting a Russian vine on one side and *Clematis montana* on the other, even an unsightly concrete garage can be transformed into a garden feature.

Wisteria sinensis. The Chinese wisteria will add a dignified charm and beauty to any building. Though several years will pass before you are able to enjoy the fragrant deep lilac flowers they are an experience worth waiting for. You must train the branches like an espalier horizontally along the wall. The flowers open in early May so you can extend the season by planting lavender and the hardy Fuchsia 'Mrs Popple' which bloom from mid summer into autumn.

Suitable groups for a mixed border

Some plants will not survive if you try to grow them in a lime soil. Rhododendrons, camellias, some heathers and gentians are examples of plants which must have an acid soil, others prefer a limey medium. All plants will be content in soil which has a pH of around 6.8.

Though the chemical character of a soil can be changed you will be well advised if your soil is naturally full of lime to choose only those plants which are tolerant of alkaline conditions – there is a wide enough selection.

Plant groups to grow in a lime soil

All the cherries will grow in a lime soil, from the neat almost bush-like Fuji cherry to the tree types like 'Kansan'. One form of the Fuji cherry – *Prunus* 'Moerheimi' – makes a neat, dome-shaped, rather wide-spreading tree whose pale pink flowers open in April and May. You could plant underneath a mixture of spring bulbs: snowdrops to flower in February, *Crocus* 'Blue bird' whose dark blue and white petals compliment the pink of the cherry blossom, followed by *Chionodoxa* 'Giant hybrids' to carry colour into early May. All the bulbs are planted in early autumn.

On one side of the group plant the soft-yellow-foliaged cone-shaped conifer *Chamaecyparis lawsoniana* 'Lutea Nana' which takes twenty years to grow 6 feet (2 m) high. This will be a feature in the garden all the year round.

Geranium endressii 'A.T. Johnson' grows only to 12 inches (30 cm) and has a succession of pink flowers throughout the summer. Autumn is catered for if you include *Sedum maximum atropurpureum*. The purple leaves of this plant are decorative during the summer and are surmounted by the dark red flowers in September and October.

The shrubby cinquefoils – forms of *Potentilla fruticosa* – grow in the wild in lime soils, so you would be quite safe in planting them in the same conditions in a garden. The choice of height and shape of a bush ranges from the modest spreading varieties like 'Elizabeth' or 'Longacre' to the 6 foot (2 m) 'Katherine Dykes' and silver-foliaged 'Vilmoriniana'. Except for the varieties 'Day Dawn' (salmon pink) and 'Red Ace', the flowers are in shades of yellow and cream. As the shrubby cinquefoils will bloom from May to October they are a useful pivot around which to design another group.

'Katherine Dykes' with flowers of good substantial yellow, *Pulmonaria* 'Munstead Blue' with the deep yellow *Narcissus* 'February Gold' growing through it will be beautiful in April and early May. *Santolina chamaecyparrissus*, an 18 inch (45 cm) high mound of grey foliage which seems to increase in its intensity with the lime content of the soil, can be allowed to mingle with *Campanula garganica* whose blue star-shaped flowers are in evidence from May to September. To give depth to the design with contrasting shape you could include *Sedum spectabile* 'Meteor' which grows 12 inches (30 cm) tall and has deep red flowers in September over grey-green fleshy leaves.

Because all the other plants lose their leaves or die down in winter plant *Hebe buxifolia* to make a perennial dark green hummock, even in the depths of winter.

You will find also that the many varieties of common lilac –

Syringa vulgaris – thrive in a lime soil, especially if they are given a position in full sun. On the shady side of the lilac you could plant *Doronicum* 'Spring Beauty', the yellow flowers on 12-inch (30 cm) stems are in bloom most years during March. *Berberis candidula*, a compact evergreen bush up to 3 feet (90 cm) high, is just the right shape to go with the upright habit of the lilac. Large single yellow flowers appear in May and are faintly fragrant. A group of the deep-blue-flowered *Scilla sibirica* 'Spring Beauty' will add another colour tone in April.

There is a lot of truth in the statement that the best plant groupings happen by accident. A design may be carefully planned, but then a plant seeds itself or is casually added to the group because there is no room elsewhere and the improvement is immediate and obvious.

For a central feature in a lawn the design must be contrived to present an harmonious appearance from every side. Escallonia are useful for this type of island site planting, they are evergreen and will stand hard pruning even in maturity. The hybrids with the prefix 'Donard' – 'Beauty', 'Brilliance', 'Gem', 'Radiance', and 'Star' – are good garden plants, growing up to 6 feet (2 m) tall they flower freely during late spring and early summer. Yellow or dark red tulips will show to advantage planted near the evergreen foliage of escallonia. You can lift the tulips at the end of May and replace them with pink or yellow antirrhinums. For the winter months *Viburnum* 'Dawn' will open a succession of pink sweetly-scented flowers from October as the antirrhinums die out until April when the tulips begin to flower.

One feature which contributes so much to the beauty of our gardens in spring is forsythia. A 5-foot ($1\frac{1}{2}$ m) bush covered in rich yellow flowers in April is a heart-warming sight. Where space permits you could include a bush of that other popular shrub the flowering currant, *Ribes sanguineum* 'King Edward VII'. If you allow the outer branches of the two bushes to overlap then the crimson of the ribes is intensified against the yellow forsythia. Both will stand hard pruning so there are no problems about restoring the balance if the growth becomes a thicket.

Narcissus 'Duke of Windsor' with white and apricot flowers is a strong growing bulb for naturalizing around the ribes. *Elaeagnus pungens* 'Maculata' is a handsome evergreen with each leaf banded down the centre with gold. Any of the summer-flowering herbaceous plants with blue flowers could be added to the group. Low growing delphiniums, campanula, asters or the *Eryngium variifolium* will look well against the gold and green elaeagnus. When you garden a soil which is well drained, carpet the ground at the front of these with mauve aubretia and blue *Muscari armeniacum* which will be in bloom with the forsythia.

Additional list of shrubs and herbaceous plants for lime soil

Shrubs

Berberis all grow well.

Ceanothus has blue flowers; there are both evergreen and deciduous forms.

Cotoneaster. The low-growing species are very good ground cover.

Cytisus (Brooms) are quick-growing shrubs which survive in poor, very dry conditions.

Genista (Gorse), like the cytisus puts up with hot dry banks.

Hypericum (St John's wort) is more versatile than most shrubs as it flowers in sun or shade.

Philadelphus (Mock orange), noted for its sweetly scented flowers, flourishes even in very shallow chalk soil.

Herbaceous

Achillea all do well; they are red- and yellow-flowered.

Anaphalis is a useful foliage plant with grey leaves and yellow flowers.

Aquilegia are easily raised from seed. There are many different shades.

Asters have popular forms; they are better known as michaelmas daisy.

Dianthus (Pinks) are longer lived on a limey soil than on acid or badly-drained clay.

Helianthus (Sunflowers) have golden flowers in late summer.

Iris. The flowers, although they do not last long, offer a wide variation in colour.

Plant groups to grow in an acid soil

These can, of course, include many of those which thrive on lime.

Rhododendrons only survive where there is no lime, but a choice can be made from varieties only 4 inches (10 cm) tall to those which, over the years, will reach tree stature. In the more exposed places grow the hardy hybrids which have been well tested.

For the small garden rhododendron 'Blue Tit' forms a neat compact bush up to 3 feet (90 cm) high, covered during April and early May with lavender blue flowers. It goes well with a ground planting of the bronze-foliaged heather *Calluna vulgaris* 'Inshriach Bronze'. The leaves are lime-green when the rhododendron is in flower, turn to gold in summer, then to bronze during the winter. The autumn-flowering *Crocus speciosus* look in keeping with this group. Lilac-blue flowers whose yellow anthers are tipped with scarlet appear just as the heather foliage takes on a bronze tint. If you prefer a brighter flower colour in rhododendrons you may like to plant the scarlet-blossomed 'Elizabeth' which has the happy habit of developing a second, smaller crop of flowers in August.

Where shelter can be given from the worst weather you can grow the larger-leaved hybrids. In a small garden exercise some restraint because the solid bank of dark-leaved rhododendrons can make a gloomy view in mid winter. There are dozens of varieties to choose from but the following are reliable – 'Britannia' (scarlet), 'Goldsworth Orange' (pale orange–yellow), 'Pink Pearl' (pink), 'Mrs G. W. Leak' (light pink with a purple brown blotch in the throat of the flower), 'Unique' (pale yellow tinged with pink), and 'Susan' (lavender).

All the hybrid rhododendrons look superb planted round with bulbs: the white-flowered daffodils 'Mount Hood' and 'Beersheba' or the deep yellow 'King Alfred'. The dog's tooth violets – *Erythronium dens-canis* – enjoy the same leafmould soil in which rhododendrons thrive. The lily-like pale pink flowers of the violet are open in March and April above attractively marbled leaves. Snowdrops and the closely akin 'summer snowflakes' (*Leucojum*) flower well in the moist soil. *Colchicum* or 'naked ladies', so difficult to place in the garden, show their chalice-shaped flowers, pink, lilac or white, to advantage against the dark green rhododendrons in September and October.

Azaleas which lose their leaves for the winter can, if you choose the right varieties, give two displays in a season. The best of these is the honeysuckle azalea – *Rhododendron luteum*. Their yellow, tubular, sweetly-scented flowers open in May; then in October the leaves turn scarlet. The annual leaf fall builds up a soil which suits many lilies. *Lilium martagon*, *L. speciosum*, and the Bellingham hybrids will grow and naturalize. The biennial hybrid foxglove – *Digitalis purpurea* 'Excelsior' – intermingled amongst the azalea will flower during the summer. Sow the foxglove seed in May, allow them to grow on during the summer and transfer the roots to their flowering positions in September.

One of the most lovely foliage plants *Acer palmatum* 'Atropurpureum' is more content when growing in acid soil. A position sheltered from cold winds is best so that the bronze red leaves develop their full beauty. *Magnolia stellata*, whose white flowers open in April as the maple leaves develop, also likes a moist acid soil. Around the group you might plant the lady's mantle – *Alchemilla mollis* – which makes a good weed-suppressing ground cover and possesses lime green flowers, and *Hosta* 'Albomarginata' whose white-margined leaves and lilac flowers will supply colour during the summer. Both of these die down completely in the autumn.

You will not feel enthusiasm for being out in the garden during the winter, but you will find days warm enough to make even the most reluctant gardener venture out. There are plants, including shrubs, which flower during the coldest part of the winter and the picture they present brightens the coldest day. *Hamamelis mollis* 'Pallida' is one of the best witch hazels, only really healthy when grown in acid soil. Pale yellow-scented flowers start to open in February and last several weeks. In good soil they will grow up to 8 feet (2.20 m) high, and in some situations the leaves colour primrose yellow before they fall. Though the flowers are a similar colour, another shrub, *Mahonia japonica* looks well in association with the witch hazel. The glossy evergreen leaves are in themselves attractive and the yellow flowers whose scent is so nearly identical with that of lily of the valley, open to overlap with those of the witch hazel. Early crocus, snowdrops, and the blue varieties of *Anemone blanda* make a beautiful underplanting to the shrubs.

Tradescantia virginiana 'Osprey', a herbaceous plant, has white flowers flecked with blue which keep on appearing from June to October. The majority of gentians, lovely though they are, nearly all need an acid soil so those which flower in autumn could be included in this group. *Gentiana macaulayi*, which grows 6 inches (15 cm) high, makes a carpet of blue flowers in August and September; *G. sino-ornata* whose blooming period continues into October, can carry on the blue theme.

People who garden an acid soil can make a labour-saving garden with a continuous display of colour by growing a mixture of heathers and dwarf conifers. Suitable conifers would include *Juniperus sabina*

'Tamariscifolia', a ground-hugging mid-green-foliaged conifer which no weed would ever succeed in penetrating, so tightly are the tiers of branches packed together. *Juniperus x media* 'Pfitzeriana Aurea' is a medium-sized conifer with horizontal branch arrangement and young yellow growth. *Chamaecyparis pisifera* 'Plumosa Aurea' again has yellow foliage, but the shape is upright and conical.

Heathers for all seasons

Erica carnea 'Myreton Ruby' has glowing red flowers from February to April on 6–9 inch (15–25 cm) stems. 'Springwood Pink' and 'Springwood White' are the same height but come into flower a month earlier.

Erica hybrida grows taller, up to 18 inches (45 cm) and carries long spikes of pink flowers from December to April.

Erica erigena 'Brightness', 24 inches (60 cm) high, is a shapely plant with red flowers open from March to May.

Erica x praegeri 'Dawn', with rose pink flowers and orange tips to the young growth, is most attractive.

Erica vagans 'Mrs D. F. Maxwell' is in the top flight of flowering shrubs, only 18 inches (45 cm) high, the spikes of deep rose flowers cover the dome-shaped bush from July to September.

Calluna vulgaris 'H. E. Beale' and 'Peter Sparkes' both produce spikes of pink fully double flowers from late August to October. Growth is fairly upright between 18 and 24 inches (45 and 60 cm). Some hybrids have delightfully coloured foliage; *Calluna vulgaris* 'R. Chapman' has golden foliage which turns orange in winter, while *Calluna vulgaris* 'Multicolor' with prostrate branches provides a foil with leaves which colour shades of red, yellow and orange. A special list is not really necessary as most will grow well in acid soils if the pH is not below 5.5 to 6.

7. Roses

Roses are a typical example of a popular garden plant which will grow in most soils, acid or lime. So often the HT and floribunda roses are depicted as formal bedding plants and they are well suited for this purpose because of their long flowering season. There is a place for every type of rose, bush or shrub, planted as specimens or in small groups down the mixed border. By using this method the roses can be brought into close association with other plants which enhance the beauty of their flowers.

Pre-planting cultivation is the same no matter where the bushes are grown. Dig the soil over 15–18 inches (35–45 cm) deep, mixing in well-rotted manure, compost or moist peat mixed with coarse bonemeal. Do this in the autumn, and leave the surface rough to weather down into a friable condition for planting the roses in February.

Order the varieties required from the nursery early. This is the best insurance against having to make another selection because the first choice is sold out. You may not have everything ready for planting when the roses arrive. Dig a shallow trench in a sheltered place, lay the bushes in this at an angle of 45 degrees, then cover the roots with soil up to the base of the branches. Trees, shrubs or roses will keep in good condition for several weeks during the dormant season 'heeled' in as described. Should the soil be frozen when the bundle arrives, just loosen the top of the packing to allow air to get in, but leave the roots wrapped after making certain they are not dry.

Planting is a simple operation. You dig out a hole deep enough and of a sufficient width to accommodate the roots. Trim any damaged roots to sound wood, the rest you can just lightly tip. Nipping the ends from the roots causes them to grow a mass of new roots which is just what they need to get away to a good start. Bury the junction between root and stem not more than 1 inch (2 cm) below the soil surface, firming the soil as it is replaced but leaving the surface loose so that moisture can penetrate easily.

Shrub roses need only a light general pruning once established. In the first year, however, top the branches back by about half. This lessens the amount of work the roots have to do until they take hold in the soil again. It is best to cut any weak twigs away at the base.

Newly planted HT and floribunda roses also need hard pruning. Remove all the unwanted wood – dead, diseased or weak growths.

You prune those which are left by three-quarters (three or four buds up from the base of the shoot). This may seem closely akin to murdering the bushes, but growths from this will be strong and vigorous, laying the basis for a healthy, disease-free bush. In subsequent years prune according to the size of bush. By just tipping back the shoots you will get a fairly tall bush which flowers a good ten days earlier than those which are hard pruned. Always cut to an outward-facing bud, and all weak or diseased shoots must be cut out completely whether practising hard or light pruning.

Rambling and climbing roses

In the first year you should remove all weak shoots and cut the remainder back to within 30–36 inches (75–90 cm) of soil level. In subsequent seasons ramblers are pruned immediately the last flower fades, taking out all shoots that carry flowers and tieing in young growths to replace them. Climbing roses are pruned in the dormant season when you have time to remove all non-productive wood almost to the base. This makes strong young shoots grow from below the cut, which can be tied in to replace them in due course. Weak growths should be cut to within two or three buds of the base. The strong shoots that are left are cut back by about one-third, just enough to remove the unripened part of the shoot which could be infected very easily by fungus disease.

Roses grown in beds or borders need regular dressings of fertilizer. Where manure or compost is in short supply mix the selected fertilizer with peat in the ratio of one 5 inch (12 cm) potfull to six 5 inch (12 cm) potfulls of moist peat. This feeds the plant and acts as a moisture-conserving mulch. To keep the bushes producing flowers throughout the summer give them a dilute liquid feed in early July.

Greenfly are sometimes a problem so spray immediately you see them. Use a systemic insecticide or derris. Mildew which shows as a white powder on the leaves, should be sprayed with a mildew specific according to the makers instructions at intervals during the season.

Recommended varieties of roses

Some most interesting grouping can be devised using roses as the central feature. On a wall the climbing rose 'Handel' with cream coloured flowers tinged rose pink at the petal edges looks most effective growing with a background of dark green ivy, *Hedera helix*

'Green Ripple'. 'Danse du Feu' needs something to soften the rather violent orange of the flowers which the dark leaved *Garrya elliptica* does admirably. In winter the garrya, particularly the male form, has long silver grey catkins.

On a low wall where the flower trusses can be trained up and allowed to arch over, the old favourite 'Ena Harkness' is worth a trial. The crimson flowers look lovely bedded round with *Senecio greyii* and the purple-foliaged red mountain spinach – *Atriplex hortensis* 'Rubra'. The senecio has grey leaves and bright yellow flowers during June, July and August while the atriplex can be sown direct and will grow 4 feet (1.20 m) high in the course of a summer.

The rambler roses tend to be more rampant growers and are best allowed to spread over a fence, outbuilding or up a tree. They are particularly desirable if grown in close proximity to *Clematis montana rubra* which flowers in spring.

The shrub roses are useful in the mixed border. 'Buff Beauty' grows 4 feet (1.20 m) high, has flowers of apricot and deep yellow which blends well with the silver-foliaged artemesia and the blue-flowered nigella (better known as love in a mist).

'Kassel' is a very dominant coloured rose, the raspberry red flowers need a natural background, and the *Nicotiana* 'Lime Green' performs the function admirably. Seeds of the nicotiana must be sown indoors in February to flower at the same time as the roses.

The hybrid tea roses are more suited to a regimented, more formal style of planting, a terrace background edging a paved or gravel walk. 'Alec's Red' is an upright-growing specimen which looks effective with the grey-leaved, blue-flowered *Lavendula* 'Hidcote'. 'Grandpa Dickson' is a pastel-shaded yellow rose which needs a strong contrast, and the dark purple heliotrope 'Marine' supplies this. Sow seeds of the heliotrope under glass in February for planting out in late May.

A most effective combination of reds and pinks is achieved by growing the vigorous pink rose 'My Choice' with dark red *Coronette Antirrhinums* and the grey-leaved *Hebe colonsi* 'Glauca'. The antirrhinums grow 12–15 inches (30–40 cm) while the shrubby hebe, just a little taller at 24 inches (60 cm), has pleasant grey leaves. If you have extra space include one of the blue-and-red-flowered hardy fuchsia.

Floribunda roses are less stiffly formal than the HT. Some of the taller varieties can hold their own as shrubs and if lightly pruned will grow up to 6 feet (2 m) high and flower from June until October. There are several with brilliant orange flowers which are excellent value when planted against a dark-leaved hedge or shrub. 'Fred Loads' with slightly fragrant, single orange flowers grows 6 feet (2 m) tall by 4 feet (1.5 m) across and 'Orange Sensation' with semi-double, damask-scented vermillion flowers grows 36–40 inches (90 cm–1 m). The mid-green feathery foliage of *X Cupressocyparis leylandii*, often used as a hedging plant, is suitable background to both roses, with *Nepeta* 'Six Hills' in the foreground. Nepeta, commonly known as cat mint grows about 24 inches (60 cm) tall with grey green leaves and lavender blue blossom.

Pastel shades are not so difficult to accommodate in a small garden as the stronger, more assertive reds. 'Dainty Maid' is a variety with deep pink single blooms with yellow stamens and when lightly pruned will grow 4½ feet (1.40 m) tall. *Iris sibirica* 'Blue Lagoon' is a good contrast in colour and shape. To extend the season of interest plant *Paeonia* 'The Bride' which has single pure white blossom or 'Madame Calot' whose double pink blooms change with age to white. In the foreground have a carpet of *Viola* 'Blue Bedder' under-planted with *Scilla* 'Spring Beauty'.

'Chinatown', 'Norwich Gold' and 'Sandringham' are three tall floribunda with predominantly yellow blooms. All look beautiful with *Thalictrum aquilegifolium* which grows 24–30 inches (60–75 cm) high with grey blue leaves and purple flowers, and the old-fashioned double red *Paeonia*. To carry the display into the winter the dark gold leaved *Thuya occ*. 'Rheingold' is ideal.

Floribunda roses do not offer a wide choice of varieties with deep red flowers. 'Heidelberg' is probably the tallest at 6 feet (2 m) and gives a profusion of full double crimson blooms throughout the season. 'Europeana' at 40 inches (1 m) carries such enormous heads of dark crimson flowers that the branches arch over under the weight of them. *Elaeagnus ebbingii*, a most elegant silver-leaved evergreen, is a suitable compliment to the crimson roses. Seed of mignonette and the creamy yellow limnanthus can be sown to carpet the ground underneath the shrubs.

By incorporating roses into the overall garden plan instead of considering them as an individual unit you get far better value from the infinite variety of shades which this most beautiful of garden flowers offers.

8. Fruit

The amount of space which can be devoted to fruit growing must be governed by the size of the garden. Decide how much space you need to provide a year-round supply of vegetables. Any garden left over can be given over to the cultivation of strawberries, black-currants, apples and any other fruit that fancy dictates or space permits. Before embarking on a really ambitious programme make sure you have enough time to do the work involved without becoming that by no means rare animal, a garden slave.

Unlike vegetables, fruit trees – apples, pears, plums and cherries – can be made into a garden feature. Pink apple blossom against the blue and white background of a May sky is one of the loveliest pictures a garden can produce.

In a very small garden tree, or top, fruit can be grown on the walls of the house or boundary fences. By choosing trained forms of top fruit as opposed to free-growing trees which take up a great deal of space you can grow a number of different varieties. The initial cost of trained forms of fruit trees compared to bushed or standard is considerably greater.

Usually there is little choice of position. You have to accept whatever soil or situation goes with the house. Ideally the site should be open and sunny without being exposed to strong winds. Sheltered gardens at the bottom of a valley are protected but can prove to be frost pockets. Frost runs downhill to pool in the hollows just like water, so that on cold, still, frosty nights trees in blossom half way up a hill are undamaged while those in the valley may have every flower blackened. In spite of the hazards you can grow good fruit in all but the worst exposed areas.

You must thoroughly prepare the soil before any planting is done. Once the garden has been planted, deep digging is inadvisable as it is likely to damage the roots.

When time permits and the garden is of reasonable size you would be well advised to double dig (pages 6–8). Work in well-rotted compost, manure, peat or similar rottable organic matter into the soil 15–18 inches (35–45 cm) deep and you have immediately laid the foundations for success. *Fresh manure* should not be placed in contact with the roots of newly planted fruit trees or bushes, as it may scorch them.

Make a pH test to discover how much lime the soil contains

(page 10). The ideal to aim for is a soil just below pH 7. Acidity can be corrected by dressings of lime. Soils containing an excess of lime can prevent the crop obtaining essential minerals; they can be improved with dressings of organic matter and certain fertilizers. You maintain the fertility of the soil after planting by mulching with rotted manure, compost and fertilizer such as 'Growmore' or fishmeal.

Good drainage is of the same importance in fruit-growing as it is in vegetable-gardening. A waterlogged soil is cold, root growth is poor, the trees starve and become susceptible to disease. You must improve the drainage by laying down pipe drains if necessary or by breaking up the subsoil as described on page 8 if this is the cause.

Do make sure the soil is free from perennial weeds before planting: strawberry and raspberry beds are hard enough to keep clean even in weed-free land, but with the weeds already established before they are planted it is nearly impossible.

Buying fruit trees

Go to a reputable nurseryman whose stock is true to name, free from disease and reasonably priced. This is a tall order, but to stay in business for any length of time a nurseryman must fit these requirements.

The rootstocks onto which the different varieties of apples, pears, plums and cherries are grafted control the size and vigour of the mature tree. They also have a bearing on the age at which a tree comes into crop. The sort of root stock you choose depends on the space allocated to each tree, the training you intend to give and the type of soil. To avoid confusion this is dealt with under the appropriate heading.

Apples

For a compact tree which comes into crop early, Malling rootstock 9, 26 or 106 is suitable for planting on a good soil. Varieties grafted onto Malling rootstocks 2 or 111 give a larger tree on good soil, but only a moderate-sized tree on poor land. So, if you have a very good soil, want a small tree which crops in three years, choose the varieties you fancy grafted on Type 9 or 26. For a slightly larger tree choose Malling rootstocks 7 or 106. For a large tree choose rootstock 2 or 111.

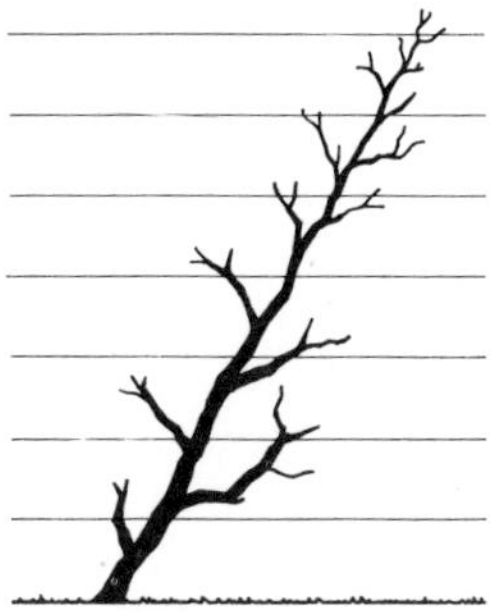

cordon

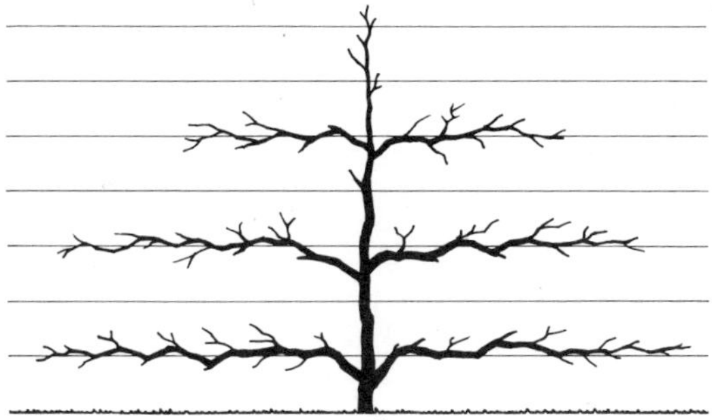

espalier

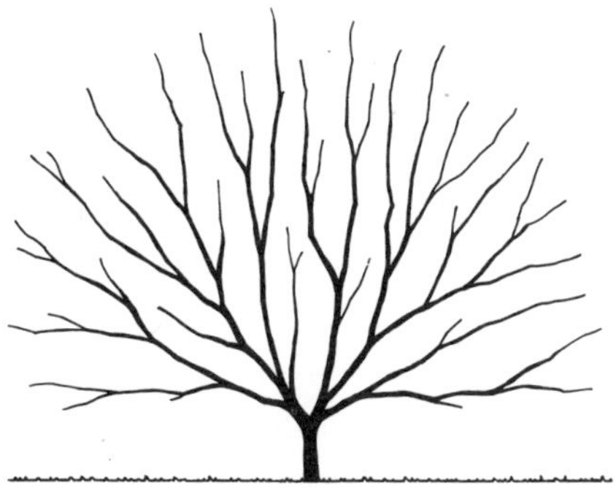

fan-trained

bush

Shape of trees

Trees can be bought to fit a particular position. A *bush* tree, as the name implies, is grown on a stem 18 inches to 3 feet (45–90 cm) high and is on a dwarfing stock, small and easy to manage. A *cordon* has a single straight stem grown on a dwarfing rootstock. Any side growths are cut hard back to make them form fruiting spurs. Cordons can be single, double or triple and are invaluable for apples and pears where space is limited. An *espalier* has a single stem with branches trained out at right angles on either side and is another useful way to grow apples and pears in a small area. *Fan-trained* is a system whereby branches of equal thickness are trained outwards and upwards from a short central trunk. A wrist with the fingers outstretched illustrates the shape of a fan-trained tree. It is mainly used for plums and cherries but apples and pears will crop well grown like this. A *dwarf pyramid* consists of a central main stem from which branches are allowed to develop at intervals in the manner of a spiral gradually diminishing in length. Again these are used mainly for apples and pears.

The different kinds of tree should be spaced as follows: bushes – 8–10 feet ($2\frac{1}{2}$–3 m) apart; cordons – 2–3 feet (60–90 cm); espaliers – 10–12 feet (3–$3\frac{3}{4}$ m); fans – 12 feet ($3\frac{3}{4}$ m); dwarf pyramids – 4 feet ($1\frac{1}{4}$ m).

Family trees are the ultimate in space saving. Three varieties of cooking or three varieties of eating apple are grafted onto one stock and grown as a single tree. For ease of management varieties should require the same feeding and pruning.

The time to plant is whenever the soil conditions are suitable between late autumn and early spring when the leaves are off the trees. Do not plant too deeply in the mistaken assumption this will help the tree; just bury the roots to exactly the depth they were in the nursery. *Stake* immediately and secure the tree firmly to it but make certain neither stem nor branches will be damaged by rubbing on the stakes. Also, make sure that the tie is not so tight that after a season or two it strangles the tree.

Pollination

Without pollination no fruit develops. Some varieties set a crop of sorts with their own pollen, others do not. To get the best crops you should plant two or more varieties which not only flower at the same time but which have pollen that fertilizes each other.

Recommended varieties

Apples are ready for eating at different times of the year. Some like 'Discovery' are ripe in late August or September, while others will keep until March or April the following year. Spread the season as much as possible by careful choice of varieties.

Recommended desert apples are: fruiting in September, 'Discovery', 'Worcester Pearmain'; fruiting in September and October, 'Epicure', 'James Grieve', 'Lord Lambourne', 'Sunset'; fruiting late, 'Cox's Orange Pippin', 'Golden Delicious', 'Winston', 'Ribston Pippin', 'Spartan'.

Recommended cookers are: fruiting in August, 'Grenadier', 'Early Victoria'; fruiting in September and October, 'Arthur Turner', 'Howgate Wonder'; fruiting late, 'Bramley Seedling', 'Annie Elizabeth', 'Lord Derby'.

Care of apples

For the first year after planting keep the trees well watered and free of weeds. A feed of 2 oz. per square yard (70 g per square metre) of complete fertilizer in March and again in mid May, plus a mulch of compost or rotted manure will keep the soil in good condition.

Pruning is vital. In the early years it establishes the framework of the tree. Later it prevents overcrowded branches yet keeps the tree vigorous, disease-free and cropping heavily.

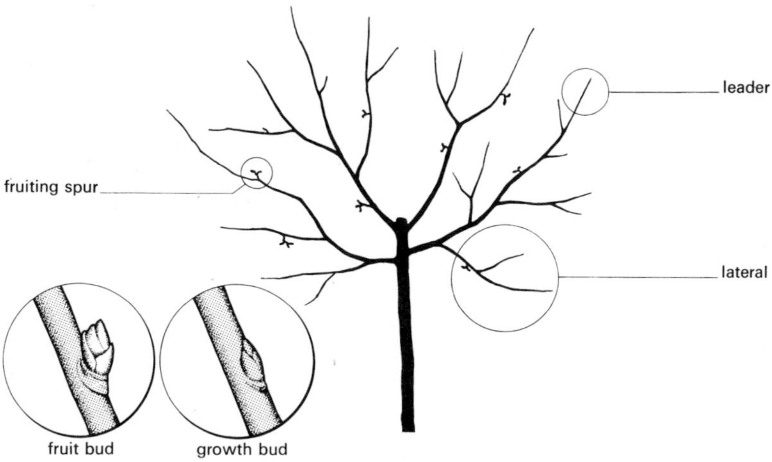

In winter remove superfluous unprofitable growth on bush trees. Shorten back the laterals (side growths which are produced from a branch) to encourage the formation of flower buds instead of growth buds. The leader (shoot at the tip of a branch) is cut back by half to a bud facing in the upward direction.

Cordons are pruned in summer – late July in the south, August in the north. Cut back all laterals growing direct from the main stem to within three leaves (not counting the cluster of small growths at the base of the shoot). Growths on spurs already established are cut back even harder to one leaf only. During winter any secondary growth from these pruned laterals or spurs is cut hard back to one leaf.

You may have to remove some of the fruit – a heavy 'set' often means the resulting apples will be small. On young trees thin the fruit to prevent too much strain being placed on the plant. The immature fruit may be cut away with scissors or twisted off between finger and thumb.

Problems of apples

Powdery mildew is a fungus disease which covers the leaves and young stems with white powder; spray at intervals from early May with lime sulphur or benomyl. These two chemicals will also control another disease which marks both leaves and fruit with olive-brown scabs. Cutting out the badly-infected wood when pruning helps control both mildew and scab. Greenfly which feed on the leaves, and young shoots, and codling moth and sawfly, which spoil the young developing apples, are controlled by spraying with fenitrothion or malathion.

Pears

Pears are not so widely grown as apples as they do not crop as well in the colder parts of the country. The trees blossom early which makes them liable to be damaged by frost so they need a position sheltered from cold east winds. Frosty winds damage the blossom and, equally important, prevent insects pollinating the flowers.

Only two rootstocks are recommended. Quince A, the best all-round stock, gives a fairly vigorous growing tree. Quince C dwarfing stock is only suitable for vigorous trees on good soils.

You must ensure that the trees are never short of moisture, so work in compost, rotted manure or peat with bonemeal added (one part of bonemeal to ten parts of peat) into the soil to a depth of 20 inches (50 cm). Each spring try to cover the soil over the roots with compost or rotted manure and a 2 oz. per square yard (70 g per square metre) fertilizer dressing.

You can get pears in trained forms – cordons, espaliers, dwarf pyramids – which are pruned like apples.

Pick the fruit when ripe; check by just lifting a pear with the palm of the hand – when ripe it will part easily from the spur. Store in a cool room until required.

Recommended varieties

'Merton Pride', in a suitably sheltered place (as an espalier on a wall facing west), produces large, well-flavoured fruit, ripe in mid September. 'Conference' ripens in late September to October; it gives heavy, regular crops but only average flavour. 'William Bon Chretien' ripens in September and has a rather unusual flavour, especially sweet if given a sheltered place; it crops regularly but should be sprayed as a routine against scab. 'Thompsons' should be grown as an espalier on a wall where the fruit ripen to full flavour in early October. 'Doyenne du Comice' has a delicious flavour but cannot be relied on to crop every year, especially in the north; it is ripe in October to November. 'Winter Nelis' produces small fruit which if kept until ripe are very sweet.

Problems of pears

Greenfly feed on young shoots causing distortion: spray with Derris or malathion. This spray also controls sawfly which are like small black slugs feeding on the leaves. Pear midge should be controlled as above. Pear scab (olive-brown spots on leaves) should be sprayed with benomyl or captan.

Plums

Plums will succeed even in moderately heavy land if it is well drained. As with apples and pears you should mulch your trees each year with compost. They do need more nitrogen so give 3 oz. per square yard (100 g per square metre) of 2:1:1 fishmeal.

Trained forms are available – fan or pyramid – but these need careful pruning to keep them in shape, so the half-standard or bush tree are the most commonly planted. Most plums only crop well if you plant two or more varieties together so the insects can carry the pollen to cross-pollinate. There are a number of rootstocks; for a small garden St Julien A is advisable. Where there is room to spare Brompton will produce a large, heavy-cropping tree. Indeed, some plum varieties crop so heavily that the branches have to be supported or they break.

Plums need little pruning beyond what is needed to keep the branches from becoming overcrowded and the tree a good shape. *All* pruning should be done in the spring after growth starts or in summer after the fruit is picked. This lessens the risk of infection from 'Silver leaf' fungus which is most active in the winter.

Do not dig around the roots after planting as this causes suckering. Keep the weeds down with 'Paraquat'-based weedkiller if hand-pulling is not practicable. When plum trees set a heavy crop you should thin the clusters down. Go over the trees in June then again after the fruit has stoned. (A natural fruit drop occurs as the stone inside the swelling fruit hardens.)

Recommended varieties

Of the early plums for eating 'Transparent Gage' and 'Victoria' are both self-fertile. 'Denniston Superb', also self-fertile, is later. 'Golden Transparent' and 'Kirkes Blue' have superb flavour but in the north need wall protection to ripen fully. Of the cooking plums 'Czar', 'Pershore' and 'Marjories Seedling' are best.

Problems of plums

Greenfly make the leaves and young shoots curl up: spray with tar oil in January to kill overwintering eggs. Malathion sprayed just before the trees blossom also controls the pest. Cure silver leaf by cutting out infected branches to clean wood and paint all wounds to protect them against re-infection. Make sure the tree is fed well. Bullfinches can strip almost every blossom bud from the trees in a few hours: netting seems to be the only solution.

Cherries

Cherries really ought to be netted. This can best be accomplished by growing the trees fan-trained on a wall. Unless you can do this it is a waste of effort growing them. To see a heavy crop of cherries being eaten piecemeal by birds before they are ripe is not a happy experience. Because growth is so vigorous there are no dwarfing rootstocks as yet, and a large wall is needed for all the sweet cherries. The acid Morello is not quite so strong and will even grow on a north wall. A fertile but not over-manured soil is best; rich soils produce an excess of wood growth and not fruit. A dressing of fertilizer – equal parts phosphate and potash at 2 oz. per square yard (70 g per square metre) – and a mulch of compost or rotted manure will be sufficient. To lessen the incidence of silver leaf prune in late summer or early spring and paint all wounds with a sealing compound as additional insurance against the disease.

Take care when picking cherries not to damage the spurs or break branches; this could allow disease to enter.

The main problems with cherries are these. Silver leaf makes leaves go pale, turn yellow and fall; cut back infected branches to clean wood and paint the cuts. Aphids (blackfly) are killed by spraying tar oil in January or malathion in the pre-blossom period.

Strawberries

Strawberries are a most suitable crop where your space is limited. Quality berries can be grown in wooden barrels with holes cut in the side. Wild strawberries flourish where the soil is well drained yet supplied with humus in the form of leaf mould. You can provide these conditions in the garden by digging the soil deeply, at the same time mixing in plenty of well-rotted manure. If the soil is heavy you just raise the bed a little above the level of the surrounding garden. A small amount of general fertilizer worked into the soil when raking the bed level for planting will help them establish quickly. Space the rows 30 inches (75 cm) apart if there is room to spare with 18 inches (45 cm) between the plants. In a small garden where each plant can be given individual attention 24 inches (60 cm) by 15 inches (40 cm) will do very well.

When planting make sure the place where the leaves and root join (the crown) comes exactly on soil level. Early September is the best time to plant, but if the runners are pot-grown April will suffice. Late-planted runners are best not cropped the first year.

See that the plants are well watered and weed-free. When you see the fruit stalk begin to arch over as the fruit swells put down sheets of black polythene, straw or special mats you can buy for the purpose. The fruit will rest on these instead of the soil and can be eaten straight from the plant without washing.

If you give strong, established plants the protection of a cloche the fruit ripens three weeks earlier than unprotected plants. By planting a number of perpetual-fruiting varieties the strawberrry season can be extended into the autumn. Small-mesh plastic netting will ensure a fair share of fruit for the kitchen and much less for the birds.

When all the fruit is picked, trim away old leaves, unwanted runners and straw and burn them but leave the young leaves and crowns undamaged. As long as the stock plants are free from virus (which shows as small leaves with yellow margins) you can get plants for a new bed quite easily. Select strong, healthy runners and peg these down to root into pots filled with John Innes or peat compost buried up to their rims down the row. In autumn the connecting stalk is cut away and the pot lifted.

Recommended varieties are 'Cambridge Rival', 'Royal Sovereign', 'Grandee', and 'Red Gauntlet'. Perpetual-fruiting varieties are 'St Claude' and 'Gento'.

Common problems are greenfly (spray with malathion) and mildew (dust with sulphur dust before blossoming).

Raspberries

These are another fruit which come into crop fairly quickly after planting. Choose a corner of the garden which is sheltered from the wind even if this means they are shaded for part of the day. It will not spoil the yield.

Dig the soil over as early as you can in the autumn including compost or rotted manure: raspberries will not put up with a poor soil. A dressing of equal parts superphosphate and sulphate of potash can be worked into the soil about two weeks before planting along the line of the rows. You can plant the bushes at any time during the winter but autumn is the best so the roots are settled before the really cold weather. Space the canes 15–18 inches (38–45 cm) apart and cut the canes hard back after planting to 9 inches (22 cm) above soil level. This helps the raspberries build up really strong stems during the summer to fruit the following year. As the canes grow tie them on to wires stretched horizontally between strong posts; space the canes out evenly, removing those which are crowded. In spring shorten back any shoot tips which show frost damage and spread compost or rotted manure down the row to keep the soil moist. After the fruit is picked cut the old canes out as close to the ground as you can get them. Keep up to eight young canes per plant and tie them in for fruiting the following year.

Propagation is a simple matter providing your plants are healthy. Just fork out the young suckers (shoots with a bit of root attached) in the autumn.

Recommended varieties are 'Malling Exploit', 'Glen Clova', 'Lloyd George', and 'Norfolk Giant'. Autumn-fruiting varieties which are pruned in spring because they fruit on canes produced the same summer are 'Zeva' and 'September'.

Common problems are greenfly (spray with tar oil in January, then with malathion just as the blossom opens), virus disease, shown by yellowing of the leaves, distortion of canes (dig up infected plants and burn them).

Gooseberries

Gooseberries are one of the easiest fruit crops to grow. The yield of berries is much heavier if you work the soil into a fertile condition by mixing in rotted manure or compost; this holds moisture during a drought. You can plant the bushes at any time when the soil is fit to walk on during autumn and winter.

Prune hard at the tips to help build up a framework of fruiting spurs. Cut the leader (shoot at the tip of the branch) back by one-third to one-half its length. Cut the side growths back to three or four buds. Once the framework is set overcrowded crossing branches, dead wood and any weak growths are also removed if they occur.

Cuttings of ripe young shoots 8–12 inches (20–30 cm) long taken in October will root if treated with rooting powder and inserted in a sandy compost. When you are transplanting the rooted cuttings rub out all except the top four buds to give a clean area of stem (leg) before branches are formed. This prevents the berries being dirtied by soil splashes.

Some fruit may be used for cooking when they are approximately half-grown. This will leave more food for the berries that are left which will in consequence be larger.

Recommended varieties are 'Keepsake', 'Green Gem', 'Whinhams Industry', and 'Leveller'.

Common problems are sawfly caterpillars which can defoliate the bushes (spray with derris), and mildew, shown by white mealy powder on shoots (spray with benomyl).

Red and white currants

These are not a very popular fruit. Where space is limited, unless they are a particular family favourite, they should be omitted in favour of blackcurrants. They will grow with the same soil preparations as gooseberries.

Cuttings 12 inches (30 cm) long from strong young shoots will root in sharp sand. October is the best time to take cuttings. Rub out all but the top four buds as with gooseberries so the bushes are on a clean leg or stem. Prune hard at first to make the bushes form spurs and cut the leaders at the tips of the branches back by half, side growths (laterals) to two or three buds.

Recommended varieties of redcurrant are 'Earliest of Fourlands' and 'Red Lake', and of white currant 'White Grape'.

A common problem is greenfly in the shoot tips: spray with 5 per cent tar oil in January or with malathion just before blossoming.

Blackcurrants

Blackcurrants are easy to grow on most soils and will yield enormous crops if you feed them. Prepare for planting with heavy dressings of rotted manure or compost; this increases both the fertility and the moisture holding capacity of the soil.

Plant at any time during the winter: October or November are the best months. Allow 5 feet ($1\frac{1}{2}$ m) of garden space to each bush; in time they get large and spreading. After planting cut *all the shoots* back to soil level. This may appear to be vandalism, but the purpose is to make a lot of shoots break from below soil level to give you fruit eighteen months later.

Mulch every year with plenty of farm manure and if the budget will permit a dressing of nitrogen as well. Blackcurrants thrive only on a rich soil.

Cuttings of young growths 8–12 inches (20–30 cm) long pushed into a sandy compost will root very easily. Leave about 2 inches (5 cm) of the tip exposed. These will be rooted enough for you to lift twelve months or so later.

Recommended varieties are 'Boskoop Giant', 'Seabrooks Black', 'Wellington XXX', and 'Malvern Cross'.

Common problems are big bud and greenfly. Big bud is caused by mites feeding in the bud which grows three or four times larger than normal: hand pick these buds and burn them to limit the pest. Spray greenfly with 5 per cent tar oil winter wash in December or January and with malathion just before the flowers open.

9. House and Flowering Pot Plants

By growing plants in the home or greenhouse you can exercise a control over the climate not possible in the open garden. Temperatures can be adjusted to suit a particular need. There are pitfalls: draughts are a hazard and can kill the delicate pot plants. Incorrect watering is the most common cause of failure, and an understanding of this essential routine is important. Too little water starves the plant of nutrient, and if persistent eventually kills through dehydration. An excess of water causes root rot and the end result is again the early demise of the unfortunate plant. When the top of the com-

post looks dry take the pot and immerse it up to the rim in a bowl of water with the chill taken off; in two or three minutes the root ball will be thoroughly and evenly watered.

The compost used by commercial growers is, of course, carefully formulated to keep the plant well fed, yet at the same time allows surplus moisture to drain away before it harms the root. The John Innes potting and peat-based mixtures supply these requirements. The type of container you use has some influence on the watering – plastic pots hold moisture longer than the traditional clay container which suffers loss of water from evaporation through the sides.

A plant in direct sunlight loses moisture at a rapid rate by evaporation through the leaves so needs watering more often than the same plant growing in shade. House plants do, in fact, prefer good but diffused light so avoid positions in full sun such as a south-facing window. In a greenhouse shade must be provided against the burning heat of a sunny summer day. Movable blinds are the most efficient and can be adjusted according to the prevailing weather. Water more frequently when the plants are in full growth.

Though conditions in a centrally-heated living-room may suit the needs of most house plants the air will be much too dry, so stand the pots in a container filled with moist pebbles, or fill an ornamental trough or jardinier with moist peat and plunge the pots in this. Evaporation will keep the air around the container comfortably humid. Sphagnum moss, moist newspaper or vermiculite serve as substitute for peat.

In due course, the plant either outgrows the pot and needs moving to a larger one or exhausts the available food. To a certain extent feeding can replenish the exhausted soil, but this is only a temporary measure. Continuous watering and feeding turns the compost very acid, root development ceases and does not start again until the plant is repotted in clean fresh material. The time to repot depends on the type of plant; just as growth commences is right as a general rule, as the roots rapidly penetrate into the new food supply when it is most needed. You can freshen plants permanently kept in the house by spraying or sponging the leaves occasionally with tepid water. In summer the pots benefit from being stood outside in showery weather.

Feed flowering plants just as the buds show colour, give foliage plants a dilute feed six to eight weeks after repotting. Always feed according to the type of plant, season of the year and state of growth; water at regular intervals, neither more or less than is required.

It may be necessary to prune excess growth, remove dead leaves, spent flowers or diseased wood. Use a sharp pair of scissors for the softer tissued plants and a well-honed knife or secateurs for the hard wood stems. If a wound bleeds treat it with an antiseptic compound – sulphur, charcoal powder or one of the proprietary compounds especially made for the purpose.

A child's interest in living plants can often be stimulated by showing how seeds of apples, oranges, lemons, etc. can be germinated and grown for several years in a pot. They do grow too large for the average living room or greenhouse, but before that time it is possible that the lemon, particularly, may have flowered or even produced fruit. Sow the seed in a standard compost in a 3 inch (8 cm) pot and place in a polythene bag in the airing cupboard. After germination the seedlings are moved out into the light and potted up individually.

How plants are arranged is important whether they are in the greenhouse or living-room. Foliage plants make more of an impact grouped together rather than dotted about the room. Dark-foliaged plants look better seen with the light through the leaves, and purple foliage takes on a richer colour tone. Yellow or silver shades are best with the light falling on them and being reflected. There are ornamental pot holders to fix to a wall which enable climbing plants to be displayed in the most natural manner.

Propagation of most house and greenhouse plants is not difficult and adds interest to indoor gardening. The techniques are dealt with in chapter 12, and the method most suitable for each plant described is given in the select list.

There are a lot of plants to choose from but the beginner would be well advised to select those with a cast-iron constitution which will survive in adverse circumstances.

Foliage plants

Asparagus plumosus 'Compactus' with feathery green foliage has been a popular indoor plant for many years. Keep it well watered in summer and only just moist in winter. This accommodating plant will stand temperatures of 45°F (8.3°C). Stock can be increased by seed sown in spring or division of the root just as growth begins in April.

Chlorophytum elatum. 'Variegatum', the St Bernard's lily is a fool-proof plant; its grass-like leaves are variegated ivory on green. In summer strawberry-like runners grow which, pegged down into compost, root and can then be detached. Take care to keep the soil only just moist in the winter.

Cissus antarctica, better known as the kangaroo vine has dark glossy green leaves which should be sponged occasionally to remove the dust. You will need to stake after the first year as the vine climbs by means of tendrils and to keep a neat shape nip out any shoots which grow in the wrong direction. These shoots root if inserted in sharp sand.

Ficus e. 'Decora', the rubber plant, tolerates quite cool, shady conditions. In winter do not over-water; in summer it needs water at least three times a week and the leaves sponged over to free them from dust. Air layering as described on pages 000–0 is the best method of propagating this plant.

Hedera canariensis 'Variegata', Canary Island ivy, is a climber which looks most attractive when grown in a pot-holder on a wall. The triangular leaves have a rich cream-coloured margin. A cool, fairly humid atmosphere is most suitable but you must not over-water or the leaves turn yellow and drop off. Tip cuttings of shoots taken in summer are easy enough to root.

Sansevieria trifasciata 'Laurentii' has sword-like leaves which are grey green, attractively marked with bands of a darker green, the margins longitudinally striped with yellow. It is an accommodating house plant which will stand quite cool temperatures so long as it is not over-watered; in either summer or winter this causes the leaves to rot off. Propagation is by dividing shoots which grow from root-like underground stems. Cut away with a sharp knife and a good section of root, they establish themselves when potted in a sandy compost.

Flowering plants

Flowering plants are, in the main, seasonal. They are brought indoors when in bloom then returned to the greenhouse as the flowers fade. As a rule they are more intolerant of poor light and fluctuating temperatures. A dry atmosphere causes flowers and buds to drop, soon followed by complete defoliation. As the flowers fade move the pots into cooler conditions but continue watering and feeding, gradually reducing the supply then increasing it again when the resting period is over.

Azalea. When buying azalea choose a plant in bud, not in full bloom, to prolong the interest. It is important that there is no lime in the water supply; when in doubt use rainwater as all azalea dislike lime in any form. Because the roots fill the pots so tightly it is difficult to get the whole pot evenly moist unless it is plunged rim-deep in a bowl of water. When in flower feed the plants at ten-day intervals, but in summer plunge the pots in peat outdoors in light shade and syringe over daily in hot weather. Cuttings of semi-ripened non-flowering shoots taken in May or June will root in *lime-free* sand.

Chrysanthemums may now be bought as flowering pot plants all the year round. The blooms stay fresh longer if the pots are placed in a cool, well-lit position. In hot weather they need watering every day, sometimes twice a day, but in cooler months twice a week should be sufficient. To induce out-of-season flowering the plants are subject to ten hours of continuous darkness to initiate bud formation. The stems are shortened by watering with a growth-retarding chemical, each plant produces a cluster of buds on the tips of the four or five side branches and these are reduced to one per branch. When you are buying a pot chrysanthemum choose one which has flowers at least three-quarters open and when it has finished flowering throw the plant away.

Cyclamen have increased steadily in popularity since they were introduced well over fifty years ago. Their pink, white or red flowers bring beauty to the home throughout the winter. Some of the new varieties have attractively marbled foliage which contrasts with the vivid petal colours. A well-lit place with a temperature of 55–60°F (13–15°C) is most suitable; they dislike a badly-ventilated location.

Keep the soil evenly moist but not too wet; indeed, it is safer to keep the roots on the dry side. As the buds show colour give a liquid feed every fourteen to twenty-one days. When the flowers fade and the leaves yellow reduce the water supply until quite dry, then turn the pot on its side for the summer. In August start the corm into growth by watering and repotting to begin the cycle all over again. New plants are raised from seed sown in February or March.

Hydrangea are a most spectacular flowering plant when well grown. Usually they are forced into bloom for sale during early spring and the colours range from pale pink through red to shades of blue. To preserve the colour intact they must be placed in a well-lit area; a west- or east-facing window is ideal. They need large quantities of water so plunge the pot up to its rim in a bowl filled with rain water, if possible, for two or three minutes, then allow it to drain. A liquid feed every ten days will also be to the plant's advantage. When flowering is finished prune the shoots back by half, or to the base if there are sufficient strong young shoots showing at soil level.

Cuttings of non-flowering shoots taken in August will root easily enough if inserted round the edge of a 4 inch (10 cm) pot which is then placed inside a polythene bag.

Poinsettia can now be bought with red, pink, cream or white bracts. Given the right growing conditions these will remain beautiful for many months – draughts, or a dry atmosphere are their worst enemies. A temperature of 55–60°F (13–15°C) in fairly good light is admirable, and you should only water enough to keep the compost evenly moist. When the flowers fade and the leaves yellow cut the stems hard back and allow the root to become nearly dry. After a brief resting period start watering again and when the shoots which appear are 4 inches (10 cm) long remove them, dip the cuttings in powdered charcoal to stop them bleeding before rooting in exactly the same manner as hydrangeas.

Pelargonium. Both regal and zonal pelargoniums are popular, easily-grown flowering pot plants with a wide enough range of flower colours to satisfy most tastes. A light position is essential during the flowering period, May to October, and they need plenty of water during the growing season. Cut the old plants hard back in October and allow to almost dry out at the roots. Cuttings can be taken in August or September of flowering shoots and will soon root in a compost of equal parts peat and sand.

Dual-purpose plants

Dual-purpose plants, though primarily grown for their flowers, have a more perennial beauty with attractive foliage or berries.

Aechmea fasciata has only recently come into favour. The common name, urn plant, gives a word picture of its very hard grey-green leaves with a hollow central tube. The flowers, at first blue then rose, grow out of this central tube or vase which during the growing season you should keep filled with rain water – a near-unique requirement. A lime-free compost is essential and this should be kept just moist, not saturated.

Small side-shoots appear around the parent plant during the summer. If you cut them away carefully and pot up in a peat-sand compost they grow happily away.

Aphelandra squarrosa 'Louisae' has beautiful dark green leaves with mid rib and veins marked out in cream. The spike-like head of yellow flowers lasts for several weeks. As flowers fade cut them away; then side-shoots develop in the junction between leaf and stem. They can be taken as cuttings or left to flower. A daily syringe over in hot weather is very beneficial. Repot each year.

Begonia semperflorens. You can easily raise begonia from seed or cuttings and because it blooms most of the year it is well worth growing. The flowers in shades of pink, red and white are carried freely on the 8–10 inch (20–25 cm) high plants. They will need water every day during the summer but rather less in the winter. Repot each year in spring. Extra plants can be raised from seed sown in the spring, or tip cuttings of young growths rooted in sand.

Beloperone guttata seems to flower most of the year. The salmon and pale yellow bracts which hide the white flowers are the reason for the popular name of shrimp plant. Cuttings of young growth taken in late spring will root in a peat-sand compost. Give a dilute liquid feed once every three weeks, and cut the flowering stems hard back in early March to encourage new growth to break.

Campanula isophylla has a more limited interest, but the pale blue or white star-shaped flowers are so appealing it is widely grown. As it is almost hardy enough to grow outdoors a high temperature is not necessary – 40°F (4°C) in winter is quite enough so long as the soil is fairly dry. Liquid feed when in flower from June to October every fourteen days. Cuttings can be taken in May.

Impatiens. The white, orange, pink or scarlet petalled busy lizzie will keep in flower most of the year. They enjoy a humid atmosphere and plenty of moisture with a liquid feed every ten days during the active growing season. Cuttings are so easy to propagate; shoots just pulled off and stood in a glass of water grow roots.

Problems with pot plants

All the plants mentioned grow in the home and greenhouse. They are only a fraction of the immense range which can be grown indoors. Problems do occur with plants grown in pots. Greenfly can be controlled with a spray of derris/pyrethrum which is quite safe to use in the home. Scale insects which look like tiny tortoises stuck on the twigs can be picked off with the point of a knife. Mealy bugs like white cotton wool can be controlled by painting them with methylated spirit. Discoloured foliage is usually a result of incorrect watering or poor growing conditions.

10. Annuals and Biennials

Annuals are plants which grow, produce flowers and set seed all in the space of one year. With a few packets of seed you can transform a desolate patch of earth into a glowing, vibrant carpet of colour. The sheer richness and diversity of choice can be utterly bewildering to anyone thinking about planting annuals for the first time.

Biennials are plants which are sown in spring, grow to maturity during the summer, flower the following year, and then die. Some real garden favourites are treated in this way – Brompton stocks, honesty, Canterbury bells and some of the evening primroses.

The largest and most important of the two groups are annuals. For the gardener's convenience they are divided into two very loose, flexible groups. Hardy annuals can be sown in the open ground direct where they are to flower. Half hardy annuals are more demanding: they need a higher temperature to germinate than the average spring affords, so they must be given the protection of a glass house during the seedling stage. Many of them can be sown outdoors in May but consequently they are not into flower until summer has passed its peak.

So often after buying a new house then fitting it with furniture there is very little money to spare for the garden – the cost of trees, shrubs, herbaceous plants and sheer economic necessity forces you back on annuals as a cheap but effective alternative.

Though most annuals will grow in a badly-prepared soil they respond to extra attention in a way that makes the effort well worth while. Dig the soil over in winter working in a quantity of rotted compost or peat. Make sure that every single weed is buried or removed, as weeding the bed is nearly impossible once the seeds are sown. Leave the surface rough to weather, then in mid April you may scatter a little fertilizer on and rake the bed level. Tread the bed firm then smooth it carefully to a seed-bed tilth with a garden rake. The ideal seed-bed has a firm base, not rock hard, with about 1 inch (3 cm) of loose soil on top to sow into.

A well-designed annual border in full bloom should have a casual natural look, so make the individual groups bold without letting any strong colour dominate. With the rake handle mark out the various blocks; if the border is designed on paper first (an interesting job for the winter evenings) marking out is easy. Set the labels in position, then draw shallow drills 6 inches (15 cm) apart for low-growing

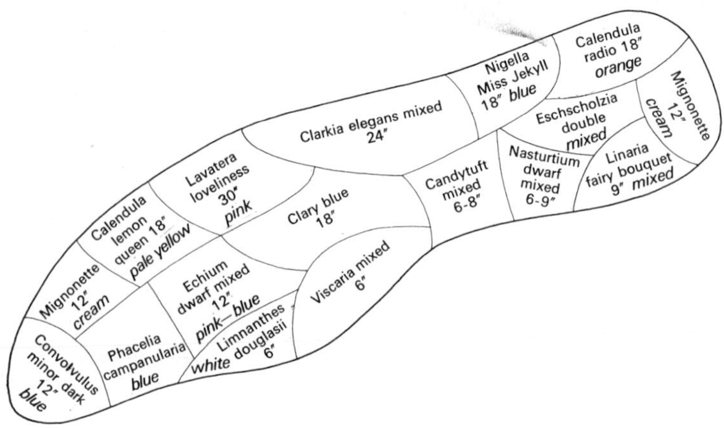

annuals, 12–15 inches (30–40 cm) for the taller-growing flowers like lavatera.

To make weeding easier it is best to sow the seed in straight rows rather than broadcast it. Sow thinly and evenly and you will not have to remove overcrowded seedlings later. If you have difficulty sowing fine seed mix it with some dry sand to assist distribution. Cover the seed by carefully raking *along* the rows so as not to spoil the straight lines, then lightly tap them firm with the back of the rake. If the weather is very dry give the bed a thorough soaking; just damping the surface is useless, it must be wet deep down using a fine spray so as not to beat the soil flat.

Except in very small borders dead-heading is a mammoth task but if you have time it will prolong the flowering period by preventing the plants from setting seed.

Hardy annuals suitable for sowing in the open

Calendula (pot marigold) 'Art Shades' has mixed colours in the orange and yellow range. Will seed themselves year after year if allowed to. Height is 15 inches (38 cm).

Candytuft 'Dwarf Fairy' forms a bright carpet of mixed colours. Height around 6 inches (15 cm).

Cornflower. Dwarf forms of 'Polka Dot' grow 12–15 inches (30–40 cm) with flowers of pink and blue.

Eschscholzia 'Californian Poppy'. To make certain of flowers all the summer sow in April and then in early June. It is lovely as an edging to a sunny border. 'Ballerina' is around 10 inches (25 cm) high, 'Monarch Art Shades' 15 inches (38 cm) high.

Godetia. The dwarf varieties make bold blocks of colour during July and August; the frilled azalea-flowered hybrids in mixed shades grow only 14 inches (35 cm) high.

Lavatera are tall plants which should be placed at the back of the border where for many weeks they are covered in deep rose trumpet-shaped flowers. About 30 inches (75 cm) high.

Mignonette. A cottage-garden favourite renowned for its sweet scent and a must for the bee keepers garden. Height 12–15 inches (30–38 cm).

Nasturtium. The dwarf forms are made to measure for the small garden and are amongst the easiest of all annuals to grow. The 'Jewel Mixture' provide a wide range of colours.

Half hardy annuals

Half hardy annuals give a better display of flowers if the seed is sown indoors during February or March. The expense of buying boxes of annuals ready for planting is becoming so prohibitive that raising your own is almost a choice born of economic necessity.

Seed may be sown in a heated greenhouse or frame, but failing these a window sill in the home makes a suitable if slightly less convenient nursery. A 4 inch (10 cm) half-pot (half the depth of a standard 4 inch (10 cm) pot) will hold enough seed. Fill the pot with John Innes seed compost or one of the peat-based mixtures so that after lightly firming there is a half inch clearance between the top of the compost and pot rim. *There is no need* for crocks, pebbles, or similar draining material. Sow the seed thinly on top of the mixture and cover with a dusting of sand or sieved compost. Germination will be quicker, more even, if the pots are covered with a pane of glass and stood in a warm dark place such as an airing cupboard. Immediately the shoots show above ground move the pots into full light. When the seedlings are big enough to get hold of they should be transplanted into standard seed trays spaced1–1½ inches (2½–4 cm) apart (hard-fingered people should use tweezers for this operation). *Never pick a seedling up by the stem – always by a leaf*. After pricking out you give the trays a thorough watering with a fine spray to settle the soil round the roots; this provides a moist atmosphere to quicken growth. In hot weather water the seedlings morning and evening.

About a fortnight before they are to be planted outdoors in late

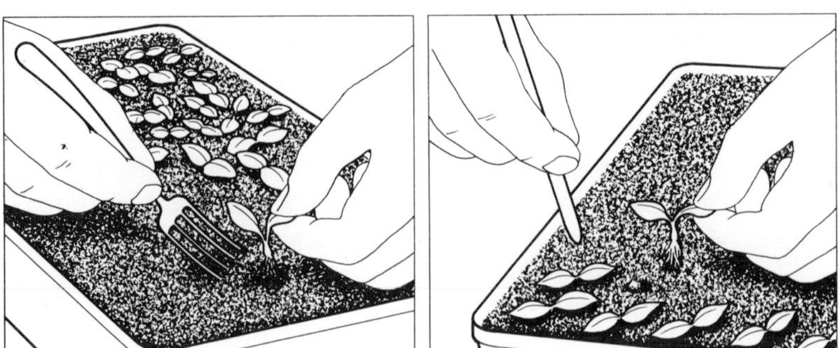

May or early June, move the boxes into frames or under cloches. This gradually hardens the plants so that there is no check to growth. Prepare the beds to receive them in the same way as for hardy annuals. If the site is occupied by spring bedding such as wallflowers and polyanthus, you should remove these and give the soil a dressing of moist peat, well-rotted compost or manure plus 2 oz. per square yard (70 g per square metre) of a complete fertilizer. Either fork this lightly into the surface or work it in with a hand cultivator.

If the soil is very dry apply water with the hosepipe to saturate it thoroughly. Once the roots are established they only need watering with a can in extremely dry weather – a hot dry climate brings the best display of flowers. Apart from keeping the weeds down and removing dead flowers they should require no more attention.

The following half hardy annuals will succeed in most soils and localities.

Antirrhinums. Probably the best-known half-hardy annual, there is such a wide choice of colour and height it is a matter of personal preference which you grow. Sow the seeds in March, prick out the seedlings when large enough into boxes, and nip out the growing tip with a pair of tweezers to make the plants bush out.

Asters. A deservedly popular annual but in some soils they are prone to disease called wilt which causes the foliage to brown. This is frequently associated with badly drained soils. The choice of varieties in all colours and heights is enormous, so you can select one, tailor-made as it were, to fit the garden. Sow the seed in late March and transplant in June to a well-drained border in full sun.

Begonia. One of the most adaptable, reliable and free-flowering bedding annuals. They are really half-hardy perennials treated as annuals for gardeners' convenience. There are plenty of different heights and colours to choose from but the F1 hybrids in named colours are good value. The seed is fine, so to get an even spread you should mix it with brick dust or dry sand. *Do not cover* except with glass and newspaper on top of the pot.

Lobelia makes a first-class edging plant with tightly-packed flowers almost hiding the foliage all through the summer. The plants grow 6 inches (15 cm) high and the colours range through shades of blue, red, pink and white. Sow the seeds in March then prick out the seedlings in threes so they make a good solid group.

Marigolds are plants for a bright sunlit bed where the intensity of colour is seen to full advantage. There are many varieties to choose from, the heights 6 inches (15 cm) to 30 inches (75 cm), so there is something to suit every garden. Sow the seed in March. To prolong the flowering season remove blooms as they fade.

Petunia have flowers like the speaker of an old-fashioned gramophone. They have been the subject of such intensive selective breeding that the range of colours and flower shape is so wide as to be confusing. Most of the F1 hybrid strains are value for money. The height is limited, only 6–12 inches (15–30 cm) which is why they are in great demand for tubs and window boxes. By using pelleted seed sown direct into boxes or peat pots pricking out is avoided. Each seed is large enough to be handled individually, spaced 1½ inches (4 cm) apart. Sow during March and remove dead flowers regularly.

Salvia. Mass-planted salvias with their brilliant scarlet flowers glowing in bright sunshine are a spectacle frequently encountered in public gardens. Seed is best sown into half pots and when large enough transplant the seedlings to peat pots. The flowers can be dark red, scarlet, salmon, pink or purple and the height 10–18 inches (25–45 cm). A well-drained soil and position in full sun are advisable.

Stocks. The combination of scent and colourful flowers does much to explain why stocks have been a well-loved annual for so many years. There are dwarf varieties, 12 inches (30 cm) high, suitable for the small garden or vigorous unbranched 'Rocket' varieties up to 30 inches (75 cm) which make good cut flowers. The 100 per cent double in shades of lavender, pink, cream, red and off-white are worth the extra money. A dressing of lime on the soil will give your plants some protection against the disease called club root which, as the name implies, distorts the root. Sow the seed under glass in March or under cloches in mid April.

Biennials

These have only limited use in the small garden because they occupy the soil for two years, only flower for a few weeks then die. Some perennials are treated as biennials and for this reason are included.

Seeds are sown in a nursery bed during late spring, early summer. When the seedlings are large enough you carefully lift and transplant them to a growing-on bed, spaced 4 inches (10 cm) apart with 12 inches (30 cm) between the rows. In autumn or spring they can be transferred to their flowering positions but you must not damage the roots or let them dry out. Leave a few plants in the nursery if you can, to replace any which the frost may kill in the flowering beds.

Canterbury bells, a bell-shaped flower, regularly featured in cottage gardens, which grow in most well-drained soils. The sturdy determinedly upright growth, between 15 and 30 inches (38 and 75 cm), does not look out of place in the mixed or herbaceous border.

Sow the seed in May to flower the following year. The dwarf variety of 'Bells of Holland' or the traditional 'Cup and saucer' varieties which are twice the height at 30 inches (75 cm) are reliable.

Honesty is grown not so much for the fragrant purple flowers but rather the silver penny seed pods. The plants grow 24 inches (60 cm) high from seed sown the previous June and are best in light shade. The seed pods make good material for dried flower arrangements and should be cut in August before they deteriorate.

Polyanthus, though a true perennial, are frequently treated as a biennial. The modern hybrids have large trusses of brightly coloured flowers carried on long stems well above the leaves. Sow the seeds in a cold frame or in boxes under a cloche during late April or May. Transplant them to grow on when large enough into a partially-shaded border which you have improved with compost or well-rotted manure. Either in October or the following March or April you can transfer them to their flowering positions and water well in dry weather.

Sweet William are attractive perennials but deteriorate after flowering to such an extent they are best grown as biennials. The flat heads of flowers are various shades of red, pink or white, often with contrasting centres. Sow the seeds in shallow drills in prepared beds outdoors, very sparsely to save thinning. In the autumn move the plants to their flowering position.

Wallflowers. This sweetly-scented biennial is an essential part of the spring garden scene. In late May sow in shallow drills in the open garden and when large enough transplant into rows 8 inches (20 cm) apart, 4–6 inches (10–15 cm) between the plants taking care not to break the tap root. Pinch out the growing tips to make them bush out. In October or March transfer them to their flowering position into soil which is well supplied with lime (acid soils should be given a dressing of 6 oz. per square yard (200 g per square metre) four weeks before planting).

11. Vegetables

Each year vegetables are becoming increasingly expensive; more and more gardeners are making a considerable economy by growing enough to supply the family needs throughout the year. A vegetable plot is not an ornamental feature so it is usually sited behind the house. Vegetables in the least accessible part of the garden also means less risk of them being stolen or vandalized.

Rotations

If you grow the same crops year after year in one particular part of the garden there is a risk of disease wiping out the whole lot. The soil becomes starved and the plants stop growing well. Avoid risks of this sort by moving each crop to a different part of the plot each year. This reduces the risk of diseases and uses up all the fertilizer residues. A simple rotation would be to divide the plot into three parts, four if potatoes are being grown.

The first year

Plot 1 grows legumes (peas, beans), onions, leeks.
Plot 2 is devoted to brassicas (members of the cabbage family which includes cauliflowers, Brussels sprouts, etc).
Plot 3 is cropped with roots, beetroot, carrots and the remaining vegetables.

The second year

Plot 1 grows brassicas.
Plot 2 grows roots.
Plot 3 grows legumes and onions.

The third year

Plot 1 grows roots.
Plot 2 grows legumes and onions.
Plot 3 grows brassicas.

The *fourth year* it will all begin again.

If you include potatoes, the plot can be divided into four sections which means the various beds only carry the same crop once in four years.

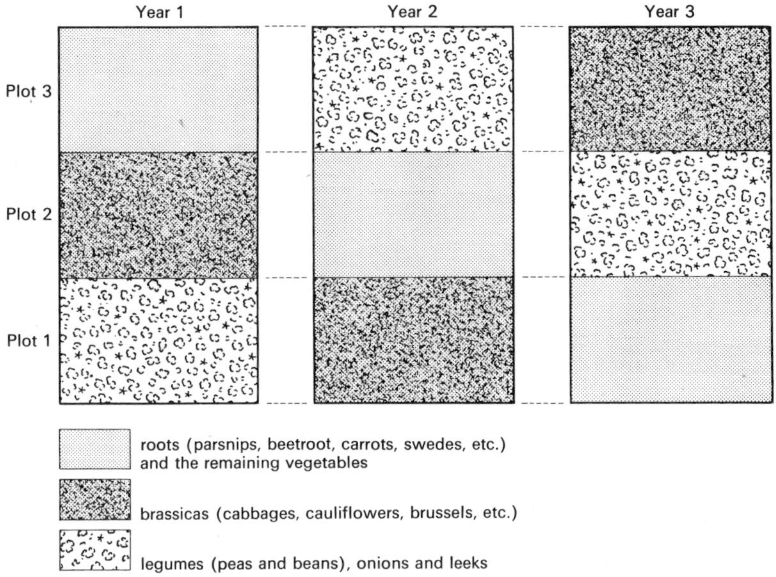

To get the very best weight of crop the soil must be kept in a good fertile condition. Dig the soil over in autumn and early winter, burying any weeds while at the same time working into the section to be cropped with legumes and onions all the compost, rotted farm manure or similar organic matter which can be spared. Potatoes are also heavy feeders so if included in the rotation the organic dressing should include their plot.

Leave the surface rough dug for the frost to penetrate. In spring when the time for seed sowing arrives a rake will quickly reduce the weathered surface to a fine seed bed.

Do not attempt to work on any soil, with the possible exception of light sand, when the weather is excessively wet. Trampling packs the soil so hard it will not work down to a fine seed bed. In spring the wind dries the soil out quickly and nothing is lost by waiting.

Breaking in a new vegetable plot either in a neglected garden or on a site recently vacated by builders may require extra work. Clear the top growth of weeds with a sickle or rotary grass-cutter then burn or compost them. Try to double dig at least part of the bed, say a third, each year. This improves the drainage, clears out the weeds and if manure or compost is worked in at the same time increases the fertility.

About one month after digging ascertain if the soil needs lime

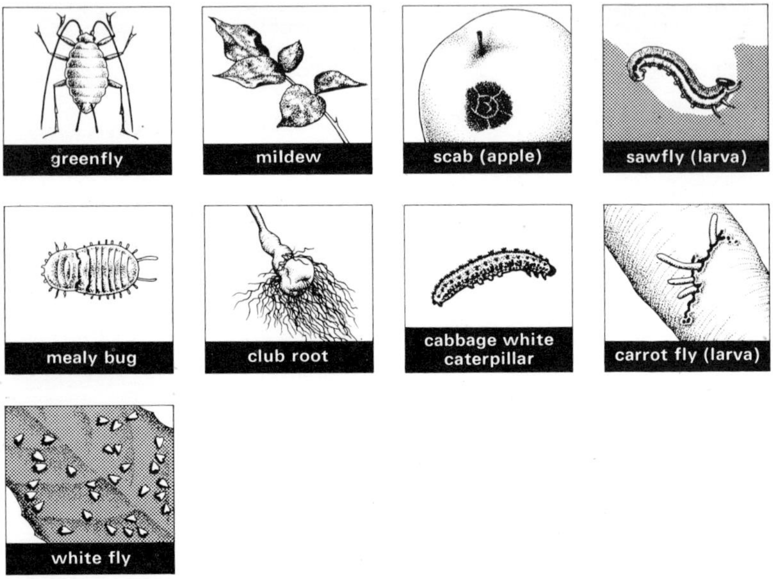

adding by doing a pH test. *Do not* apply fresh manure and lime together. Allow at least four weeks between the two operations.

Buy seeds from a reputable source, read the sowing instructions on the packet about times and depth of sowing. Do not sow too many of the same variety of vegetables at once or there will be periods of glut and famine. Rather, sow short rows at regular intervals, especially of quick maturing crops like salads. Grow more of the vegetables which the family will enjoy eating. This is an obvious point but frequently overlooked.

Potatoes

These are a good crop for cleaning and breaking in new ground. Manure the bed in the autumn, then when breaking down for planting the following spring sprinkle 2 oz. of fertilizer to the square yard (70 g per square metre). Buy good-quality 'seed' potatoes. For earlies grow 'Home Guard', 'Foremost', 'Arran Comet' or 'Ulster Chieftain'. For maincrop grow 'Majestic', 'Pentland Crown', 'Kerrs Pink' or 'Dr McIntosh'.

Stand the tubers eye-end up in a tray in a light airy place to 'chit' (grow short green sprouts) during late February. In April plant the tubers in holes 4 inches (10 cm) deep. Plant earlies 12 inches (30 cm) apart with 18–20 inches (45–50 cm) between rows. Maincrop are spaced 15 inches (38 cm) apart with 24 inches (60 cm) dividing the rows.

As the tops grow hoe between the rows to kill germinating weeds. Draw the soil up around the tops to form a ridge (earthing up). Early potatoes are big enough for eating by late June and are lifted as required for the table. Maincrop tubers for storing are dug up and allowed to dry on the surface before being placed in a frost free shed. Always keep potatoes in the dark, they turn green when exposed to the light.

Potato blight is a problem disease in some areas: spray with Bordeaux mixture in mid July.

Beans and peas

Broad beans

These are a hardy, easy-to-grow, heavy-cropping vegetable in a well-cultivated soil. Hardy varieties of longpod (Aquadulce) can be sown in a sheltered bed during October for an early crop. For these overwintering crops the soil must be well drained. The first sowings are made in double rows, 3 inches (8 cm) deep, 9 inches (22 cm) apart with 18 inches (45 cm) between the double rows. Make additional sowings until early May to give a continuity of cropping.

Push the hoe to keep the weeds down. As the bottom pods set pinch out the growing tip to deter black aphis, and dust the plants with derris.

Reliable broad bean varieties are 'Suttons Dwarf', 'Imperial White Longpod', 'Windsor' and 'Greensleeves'.

Dwarf or French beans

These need a deeply-dug soil, well manured from a previous crop and the drainage must be good or the plants develop root rot.

Seeds are sown when the soil has had a chance to warm, usually early May. If French beans are preferred to runner beans another sowing could be made two weeks after the first to give a succession. The seeds are buried 1½–2 inches (4–5 cm) deep, spaced 4 inches (10 cm) apart with 15 inches (38 cm) between the rows. Thin the seedlings after germination to 8 inches (20 cm).

Do not let any of the pods seed, and water in dry weather.

Recommended varieties are 'The Prince', 'Canadian Wonder', 'Masterpiece' or the haricot bean 'Cherrier Vert'.

Runner beans

These require a warm sheltered site to succeed and a well drained soil. Dig the site 18 inches (45 cm) deep during the winter mixing in plenty of rotted manure or compost – particularly into the lower 10 inches (25 cm).

In cold areas sow the seed in pots under glass, or direct where they are to crop under cloches. The final spacing is 12 inches (30 cm) between the plants. Unstaked plants are grown in rows 18 inches (45 cm) apart and the growing points are pinched out to make them bush rather than climb. Climbing plants are supported on canes or nets.

Water in dry weather, and when picking begins liquid-feed every ten days. Suitable varieties are 'Prizewinner' and 'Achievement' (staked) and 'Kelvedon Marvel' and 'Dwarf Scarlet' (unstaked).

Root rot is avoided by changing the site for the beans each year. Spray blackfly with derris.

Two methods of supporting runner beans

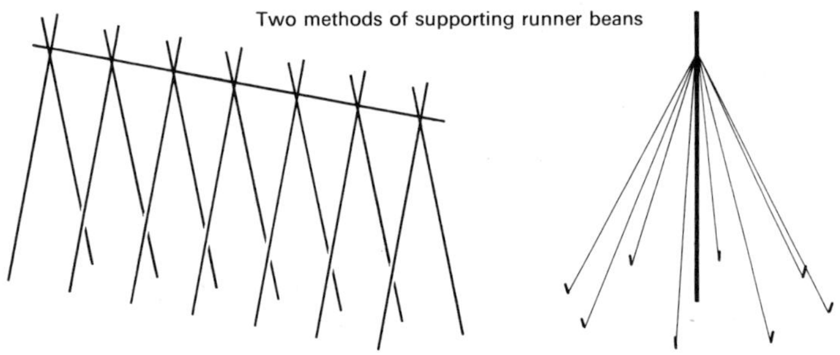

Peas

Like runner beans, peas enjoy a soil which has been well manured the previous winter. A rich, moisture-retentive soil produces a heavier crop of pods.

Seed of early varieties may be sown under cloches during February on light soils and March in colder areas. Further sowings at twenty-day intervals until mid-June will keep up a succession of cropping throughout the summer.

Take out a shallow trench 2 inches (5 cm) deep and 8 inches (20 cm) wide. Sow the seeds in this 3 inches (7–8 cm) apart each way. Distance between the rows is varied according to the variety, with 24 inches (60 cm) as a maximum when they are staked.

A mulch of peat, straw or lawn mowings between the rows helps to conserve moisture. Suitable varieties are 'Little Marvel' (where space is limited make successional sowings of this variety from March to mid June instead of using taller varieties), 'Feltham First' (grows to 18 inches, 45 cm), 'Early Onward' (20 inches, 50 cm), 'Green Shaft' (24 inches, 60 cm), 'Onward' a reliable variety in all areas at 24 inches (60 cm).

There should not be any problems in well-prepared soil.

Brassicas (cabbage family)

Spring cabbage

A well-drained soil and sheltered position is best as this crop stands out all winter. Sow seeds in a nursery row in July (in the north) or early August (in the south). Transplant the resulting seedlings into the cropping position in September or October so the roots have time to establish before the cold weather starts. Space them 15 inches (35–40 cm) apart each way.

Run the cultivator through the rows to let air into the soil. In late March give a dressing of high-nitrogen fertilizer to make the leaves grow quickly so they are tender. Suitable varieties are 'Harbinger', 'Durham Early' and 'Offenham'.

Summer cabbage

Summer cabbage need a well-manured soil so that they grow to maturity quickly. Cultivate the soil in winter, working in manure or compost and leaving the surface rough to weather. Sow seed indoors in February, outside in seed beds in early April. Transplant when large enough to cropping area, setting the plants out 15 inches (35–40 cm) apart each way. Water heavily in dry weather. Suitable varieties are 'Winningstadt', 'Maystar' and 'Cannon Ball'.

Winter cabbage

Sow seed in May to give plants for lining out into the plot left vacant when the new potatoes are lifted. Space them 18 inches (40 cm) apart with 24 inches (60 cm) between the rows. Suitable varieties are 'Winter White', 'January King' and 'Christmas Drumhead'.

Savoy and kale

Both require a soil which has been well cultivated but not freshly manured. Sow seed in May to early June. In late July to early August the seedlings are transplanted to the permanent bed which is prepared with a fertilizer based on phosphate and potash applied at 2 oz. per square yard (70 g per square metre). Space them 18 inches (45 cm) apart either way and firm well after planting. Suitable varieties are 'Best of All' and 'Rearguard'.

Brussels sprouts

These succeed best in land which is well drained as they will be cropped throughout the winter. As with savoys, work in a fertilizer dressing before planting, based on superphosphates and potash at the rate of 2 oz. per square yard (70 g per square metre).

Sow the seeds of early varieties in frames or under cloches in March, maincrop and lates in seed beds outdoors in April. The plants are transplanted in June, spaced at 24 inches (60 cm) square. Earth up the stems as they grow to stop the wind blowing them about.

Pick the sprouts as they mature from the base of the stems upwards. Suitable varieties are 'Peer Gynt' (early dwarf), 'Fillbasket', 'Market Rearguard' and 'Citadel'.

Cauliflowers

Cauliflowers prefer soil which has been deeply dug and well manured the previous winter. To develop strong roots work in 1 oz. per square yard (35 g per square metre) of superphosphate of lime before planting up, or 2 oz. fishmeal per square yard (70 g per square metre) if the soil is of poor quality.

Sow seeds under glass in February, also in nursery beds outdoors in April and early May. Only a few plants are required at any one time for planting up or they all mature together.

Summer varieties are spaced out 18 inches (45 cm) square, autumn varieties 24 inches (60 cm) square. They must never be short of water or starved for fertilizer or the crop will fail. Protect the cauliflowers as they form by bending the large outer leaves over them. Suitable varieties for succession are 'All The Year Round' (sown at three-week intervals these will see a family supplied through the summer), 'Snowball', 'Dominant' and for autumn, 'Barrier Reef' and 'Autumn Protecting'.

Winter cauliflower and sprouting broccoli

These need a long growing season and a soil which has been well firmed. Sow seed in May into nursery beds. Before transplanting, hoe in a fishmeal fertilizer at 3–4 oz. per square yard (100–120 g per square metre) and when the plants are large enough space them 24 inches (60 cm) apart in this prepared ground. No further feed is necessary as soft growth is quickly killed by frost.

Recommended varieties of winter cauliflower are 'Thanet' and 'Late Queen', and of sprouting broccoli 'Winter Sprouting' and 'Purple Sprouting'.

The cabbage family enjoy a fair share of problems. Cabbage root fly (legless white maggots on the roots) is avoided by dusting the roots with 4 per cent calomel when transplanting, or watering thoroughly with Lindane after planting. Club root causes distortion of the root; make sure the drainage is good, and lime the bed heavily – 6–8 oz. per square yard (200–280 g per square metre). Dip the roots in a thick paste made by mixing 4 per cent calomel with water when transplanting. Cabbage butterfly caterpillars can be hand-picked or the plants sprayed with liquid derris.

Root vegetables

Carrots

Carrots grow the best on light soils. On heavier land sow stump-rooted or intermediate varieties.

Dig the bed in the autumn, if possible 15–18 inches (35–45 cm) deep. Do not include any fresh manure for this crop. When raking down for sowing the seed, work in a dressing of 2 oz. superphosphate of lime and 1 oz. sulphate of potash per square yard (70 g and 35 g per square metre).

First sowings can be made under cloche in March, the maincrop for winter use in May. Use the early sowings while still young as they tend to split if left until autumn. Space the rows 12 inches (30 cm) apart, the distance in the row varies according to variety from 2–4 inches (5–10 cm).

In October lift and sort the roots, clean the best and pack in dry sand away from frost and use the remainder immediately.

Recommended varieties are 'Early Nantes', 'Champion Scarlet Horn' and 'New Red Intermediate'.

The major pest is carrot fly. Sow thinly and thin carefully – the smell of crushed foliage attracts the fly. Dust down the rows with weathered soot.

Beetroot

As with carrots beetroot must not be grown on freshly-manured land and require the same soil preparation plus the fertilizer dressing.

Sow the seed in drills 12 inches (30 cm) apart and 1 inch (2–3 cm) deep under cloches in April to give early roots for use in salads. To raise roots for storing the seed should be sown in early July. Thin the seedling to 4 inches (10 cm) apart when large enough to handle.

Roots for storing are lifted with a fork and the tops are twisted, *not cut*, off. Discard any damaged roots. The rest are packed in a frost free place between layers of sand.

Recommended varieties are 'Boltardy', 'Globe' and the long-rooted 'Cheltenham Green Top'.

Problems: there are usually none.

Parsnips

Parsnips are extremely hardy and can be left in the ground through the winter. Dig the intended plot over during the winter leaving the surface rough to weather, but do *not* use any manure. Sow the seed immediately the soil is fit to work in early spring in shallow drills $\frac{1}{2}$–1 inch (1–2 cm) deep. When the seedlings are large enough thin them to 6 inches (15 cm) apart. Parsnips can be lifted and stored like carrots but this is unnecessary until the plot is required for digging.

Recommended varieties are 'Avonresister' (stump-rooted), 'Offenham' (medium) and 'Tender and True' (good all round).

The major problem – is canker which shows as a rusty brown stain on the roots; if your parsnips are affected grow resistant varieties such as 'Tender and True', also practice a rotation.

Turnips

In a small garden turnips are best used as a catch crop (that is, sown into ground that has been cleared of an earlier crop). Dress the soil with a general fertilizer at the rate of 2 oz. per square yard (70 g per square metre). Sow the seed in shallow drills $\frac{1}{2}$ inch (1 cm) deep. Thin gradually until the plants stand 5 inches (12 cm) apart. Use the roots as required, any which remain you can lift with a fork, clean and store in sand out of frost danger.

Recommended varieties are 'Golden Ball' and 'Purple Milan'.

The major problem is flea beetles which eat holes in the leaves. Damp the rows over with water at dusk and dust with derris powder.

The onion family

Onions

Onions like a fertile soil so dig the bed in early winter, working in plenty of compost or manure. When raking down to a sowing tilth add 2 oz. to the square yard (70 g per square metre) of good general fertilizer.

Sow the seed in a greenhouse, frame or under cloche in February. Transplant to the cropping area in mid April, lifting the seedlings carefully so as not to damage the roots, and space them 6 inches (15 cm) apart with 12 inches (30 cm) between the rows.

Seed may be sown direct when the soil is warm enough in the spring but they will not make large bulbs for storage.

An alternative to seed is onion 'sets' (small onion bulbs). Do not use fresh manure; they are best planted to follow a crop for which the soil was well manured the previous year, such as potatoes. Increase the general fertilizer dressing to 3 or 4 oz. per square yard (100–140 g per square metre). The bulbs are pressed into the soil surface so only the tip shows. In mid August bend the tops over to quicken ripening. Lift the bulbs with a fork when the tops have yellowed and dry them in a sunny place before storing in a frost free shed.

Suitable varieties are 'Ailsa Craig' and 'Sutton Globe' for sowing under glass, 'Bedfordshire Champion' for sowing direct in the spring, 'Solidity' for sowing in autumn to overwinter, and as sets 'Stuttgarter Giant'.

Salad onion

'White Lisbon' can be sown with other salad crops in short rows to give a succession of tender young onions for use throughout the summer. Onion fly is a nuisance and any plants attacked should be dug up with the soil around them and burned. A strong solution of trichlorphon watered along the rows three times during early summer will help control the pest.

Shallots

Shallots like a similar soil to onions so soil preparation is the same. Plant the 'sets' in late February or early March when the soil is fit to work. Press the sets into the soil until only the tip is left showing. Lift the bunches of bulbs in early August and spread them out to dry. You can select the smaller bulbs for planting the following year and keep the remainder until required for eating in a frost free place.

Leeks

Leeks are a hardy crop capable of standing out all winter without being damaged by frost. They also like a fertile soil, so dig and manure the plot during the winter; or they can follow the early potatoes.

Sow the seed in March or April in a cold frame or small seedbed. When large enough, about 8–10 inches (20–25 cm) high, transplant into holes made with a blunt dibber – 6 inches (15 cm) deep, 8 inches (20 cm) apart with 12 inches (30 cm) between rows. Do not fill the hole in; a thorough watering after planting will secure the roots and if you earth up as the plants grow it will increase the length of the blanched stem.

Salad and miscellaneous vegetables

Spinach

Spinach needs a well-cultivated ground which retains moisture, so work in rotted manure or compost when digging.

Sow the seed in shallow drills in early April then again in early June to give a succession. Try to put the second sowing in the shade possibly on the north side of runner beans to avoid hot sun and water well in dry weather. Winter spinach is sown during September.

Recommended varieties are 'Greenmarket' (sow in September or March), 'Long Standing Round' (summer only) and 'Long Standing Prickly' (winter and spring).

Lettuce

Lettuce is a most important crop. The home-grown heads are so superior to those bought in a shop. The soil should be well supplied with compost or rotted manure and when raking down add a dressing of fertilizer at 2 oz. per square yard (70 g per square metre).

You can sow in frames or cloches in September to crop in spring, or under glass in peat pots in late February for transplanting to the open ground in April. Outdoors sow at eight-day intervals in short rows from early April onwards.

Draw the drills ½ inch (1 cm) deep and about 12 feet (4 m) long. When the seedlings are large enough to handle thin to 6 or 8 inches (15 or 20 cm) apart, depending on the variety.

Choose varieties to give succession. Sow 'Valdor' in September for overwintering, 'May Queen' under glass in January or February, 'Tom Thumb' outdoors in spring, 'Avondefiance', 'Buttercrunch' and 'Windermere' for general summer use.

Radish

Radish need a similar soil to lettuce so you can sow in the same bed. Sow the seed at eighteen-day intervals from early March until mid May, then again in August if required. *Do not sow in mid summer* – the roots are unpalatable.

Recommended varieties are 'Cherry Belle' and 'French Breakfast'.

Celery

Celery (trench) needs a deep rich soil. Take out a trench 12 inches (30 cm) deep and fork compost or rotted manure into the bottom, then replace the soil to within 6 inches (15 cm) of the previous level.

Sow the seeds under glass, prick these off into peat or soil blocks and harden off for transplanting to the open ground in early June. Celery needs a lot of water so hose the plants down twice a day in dry weather. Remove the side shoots and commence earthing up when the plants are 10 inches (25 cm) high. First, lightly bunch the foliage then work the soil in round the stems to a depth of 3 inches (8 cm). Take care no soil gets into the heart of the plant as it could cause rotting. Earth up twice more at three-weekly intervals.

Recommended varieties are 'Unrivalled Pink' and 'Giant White'.

Leaf miner, which causes blistering of the leaves, can be controlled by hand-picking infected leaves and spraying with malathion.

Self-blanching celery needs the same root run but is not planted in a trench or earthed up. Sow the seeds in late March, pot them into peat pots or boxes, then after hardening off plant them out 9 inches (22 cm) apart each way. By putting them in blocks rather than rows growth is erect and the stems blanch better.

Recommended varieties are 'Golden Self Blanching' and 'American Green'.

Celeriac

Celeriac is like a cross between a turnip and celery. The crop must grow quickly in well watered and matured soil or it is tough and inedible.

Dig and manure the soil in autumn, sow the seeds in March and plant out 12 inches (30 cm) apart. Remove the side shoots and any of the older leaves as they yellow. Roots may be stored in sand.

The best variety is 'Globus'.

Tomatoes

Tomatoes are always worthwhile to grow. They present few problems in cultivation. In a greenhouse the plants can be brought into crop earlier. You can plant into the existing soil of the greenhouse but if this continues for several years there is a risk of disease building up. Alternatively, plant in rings (bottomless pots) filled with sterilized compost standing on a 4 inch (10 cm) bed of ½ inch (1–1½ cm) gravel; in this case you do not water the rings only the gravel below. The third method is to grow plants in peat-filled polythene sleeves. These are specially prepared containers which can be used in the greenhouse, a spare bedroom, window sill, sunny patio or roof top garden. Large pots have the same versatility.

Sow two seeds into a peat pot; if both germinate remove one. Allow the other to grow on until the roots are right through the pot sides then plant out in the cropping position. *Do not* overcrowd the plants – it causes disease and reduces the crop – and *do not* disturb the soil ball which covers the roots. Water the roots thoroughly after planting and keep the greenhouse ventilators closed for a day or two.

No matter what growing technique is adopted the stems will need support; canes, string or plastic-covered wire are suitable but make certain they are strong enough to take the weight: up to 11 lbs. (3–4 kg) of tomatoes in full crop.

When the flowers are open at mid-day tap the plants to transfer the pollen and fertilize them. Afterwards, on sunny days, damp the foliage over with a fine spray of water. When the fruit on the lowest truss is the size of a pea start feeding every ten days with a proprietary tomato fertilizer, according to the makers' instructions. Remove all side shoots which grow from the point where the leaf stalk joins the main stem. This should be done while the shoots are still small.

As the fruit on the lower trusses is picked, remove some of the leaves, particularly those which are yellowing, to allow air circulation.

Recommended varieties are 'Moneymaker', 'Alicante', 'Ailsa Craig' and 'Golden Queen'.

Tomatoes for outdoor planting are best sown in late March into pots as for indoor cultivation. After being thoroughly hardened off in early June transfer them outdoors to a sheltered position facing due south, if possible. Dig the ground over four to six weeks before planting, working in rotted manure or compost. Ten days before the plants are installed add a dressing of 3 oz. per square yard (100 g per square metre) of a good tomato fertilizer. Space the plants 18 inches (45 cm) each way. Bush varieties will not need support, nor need their side shoots be removed; others must be both staked and side-shooted as for indoor varieties.

Put a layer of peat or polythene sheeting between the rows to keep the fruit from getting soiled. There may be fruit which has not ripened by the autumn. Pull the plants up and hang them upside down in a warm room where they will continue to ripen off.

Recommended varieties are 'Moneymaker', 'Outdoor Girl' and Ailsa Craig'. Recommended bush varieties are 'Sleaford Abundance' and 'Amateur'.

Blight, usually on outdoor plants only, causes browning of the foliage: spray with maneb or zineb at fourteen-day intervals from early July onwards. Leaf mould, usually only in greenhouses, causes yellowing of the leaves with brown mould: keep the house well ventilated and spray with zineb or maneb. Green back is shown by hard green patches on the fruit which does not ripen: shade from excess sun and give a teaspoonful of potash in water to each plant.

Cucumbers

You can grow cucumbers in pots, frames, greenhouses or in polythene sleeves. In frames or greenhouses make up a mound of well-rotted manure covered with 6 inches (15 cm) of sterilized soil. Sow the seeds two to a pot, removing one seedling if both germinate. When the roots fill the pot transfer to the cropping position.

The stems can be trained up nets or string if grown in a greenhouse, or spaced out across the floor of the frame. Pinch out the growing point when 4–6 ft ($1\frac{1}{4}$–$1\frac{3}{4}$ m) long (greenhouse) or at the fifth leaf in frame cultivation. This causes fruit-bearing side shoots to break. Females have a tiny swelling behind the flowers, the male flowers have not and are removed. Keep the plants shaded from hot sun, also spray overhead with water morning and evening in dry weather.

As the flowers 'set', nip out the tip of the lateral two leaves past the fruit. Remove any yellow foliage and top dress the roots after the first fruits are cut so the soil is not exhausted.

Recommended varieties are 'Telegraph Improved' and 'Butchers Disease Resistant'. 'Femdan' and 'Rocket' produce only female flowers. For outdoor cultivation try 'Burpless Tasty Green' and 'Baton Vert'.

Foot rot is caused by poor drainage: avoid it by growing the plants on a ridge. White fly, once established, is a difficult pest to control: alternate sprays with formothion and pyrethrum will reduce the numbers.

Marrows

Vegetable marrows need only a warm corner and rich soil to crop well – a mound of rotted compost or manure provides the ideal root conditions, or the plants may be grown on the manure or compost stack itself.

Sow the seeds under glass in early May, or direct where they are to crop later in the month. One or two plants will provide enough fruit for a family of four. Marrows should never be short of moisture so water heavily in dry weather. You can cut the fruit when they are 4–6 inches (10–15 cm) long for immediate use or leave to grow to full size and store them. Marrows hung in net bags in an airy, frost-free place but not touching each other will keep for several weeks.

Recommended varieties are 'Green Bush', 'White Bush', 'Green Trailing' and 'White Trailing', and of the dual purpose 'Golden Zucchini' and 'Courgette Improved'.

Melons

Melons come under the heading of fruit but like tomatoes and marrows are grown with the vegetables. They need a rich yet well-drained soil. The best way to provide this is to put down mounds of compost or manure and cover them with soil.

Seeds are sown in early May, two in a peat pot. The weakest should be removed if both germinate. The best place to germinate melon seeds is the airing cupboard if a heated frame or greenhouse is not available. Move the pots into full light when the shoots are through the soil. When the roots are through the pot, usually at the fourth rough leaf stage, plant in the beds. Polythene sleeves full of compost or pots are alternatives where the bed method is impracticable. Train the stems up nets or whatever support can be provided.

Pinch the growing point out at the height required and train the laterals that develop horizontally along the supports.

As the female flowers appear (they are indicated by the swollen stem behind the flower itself) they are pollinated with the ripe male flower. Try to pollinate when four females are fully open at the same time when the fruits swell evenly. Strip the petals from a male flower then press it onto the stigma of the female so it is well dusted with pollen. As the fruit swells pinch back the tip of the lateral on which it is growing to one leaf beyond the fruit. Support the fruit in a net bag or the weight will tear the stem. Begin feeding four to seven days after fertilization and continue at ten-day intervals until the fruit starts to ripen. The plants must not be permitted to suffer from drought so water twice a day in hot weather.

Melons are ripe for eating if when gently pressed with the fingers at the end farthest away from the stalk it feels slightly soft.

Recommended varieties to grow in the greenhouse are 'Superlative' and 'Hero of Lockinge', and in the frame 'Charantais', 'Ogen' and 'Sweetheart'.

Melons soon sicken if the soil is too wet or ventilation incorrect. Collar rot is a danger: ensure drainage is good. Red spider makes leaves mottled and very pale coloured. Keep the atmosphere humid; alternate sprays of derris and malathion should check the mites.

Sweet corn

A sheltered but not shaded position is most suitable for sweet corn. A dressing of rotted manure or compost should be worked into the soil prior to planting. Failing this a dressing of fishmeal at 4 oz. per square yard (140 g per square metre) raked into the plot ten days or so before planting up will suffice.

Sow the seeds under glass in April, or direct into the ground where they are to mature under cloches. The plants are transferred when they have been hardened off in late May into blocks 24 inches (60 cm) apart in the rows with 15 inches (35–40 cm) between the individual plants. It is advisable to plant in blocks rather than rows so pollination can take place more effectively. Water in dry weather. The cobs are ripe when the silk tassel at the end is brown and the sheath feels tightly packed.

Recommended varieties are 'First of All', 'Kelvedon Glory' and 'John Innes Hybrid'.

The biggest problem is our climate, but given an average summer there are none.

Herbs

A small border can usually be made available near the kitchen door in which to grow the really important herbs.

Mint

Mint roots are planted in early March but unless the garden has space to spare their growth must be confined in some way. Four paving slabs buried on their edges to form a root-tight box will do very well. By top-dressing the box each year with compost the mint will be kept from starvation.

Parsley

Make the first sowing of parsley under cloche in early March – a 6 ft (2 m) row is enough. To keep up the supply further sowings can be made in late June and early September.

Chives

Chives can also be grown from seed sown under glass in pots or boxes. After germination, harden off and plant up outside during May. You can pot up a few plants to give tender shoots for winter use.

Sage

Sage may be grown from seed sown indoors during March. Water very carefully until the seedlings establish or they may damp off. When large enough to handle pot them up to grow on before transplanting them to the open garden. Gather the sage for drying before the flower spikes open and hang the bunches in a light airy shed till completely dry before storing.

Thyme

Thyme may be sown direct into the open ground in a sunny border if the soil is light and well drained. Otherwise sow in pots and transfer them to the open garden when large enough.

Once the bushes of thyme or sage are established they can be increased by dividing the roots in March. Save the youngest shoots with a piece of root attached for re-planting.

12. Stocking the Garden

There are two methods of propagation. The sexual method uses seed and the vegetative method uses cuttings or grafting. Plants are expensive, so raise as many as possible yourself. This is where the frame or greenhouse proves a good investment as seed sown under cover has a greater chance of success. Make certain that the seed is sound and true to name by buying from a reputable seedsman.

Seed saved from a cross between two plants of the same species usually produces offspring identical with the parent. Seed saved from a hybrid shows a great deal of variation. Some of the seedlings produce flowers with the characteristics of one parent, some are like the other, while the remainder are intermediate between the two.

Cuttings, divisions, layers or grafts of species or hybrids will produce young plants identical in every way with the parent plant.

Seed sowing

Containers for seed sowing vary in shape and dimension. The most useful is a half pot 4–5 inches (10–12 cm) in diameter or one of the small plastic trays. These must be clean as hygiene is most important when handling young plants. Clay or plastic pots have drainage holes at the bottom. A piece of perforated zinc, some broken clay pot or a handful of gravel ensures the drainage hole is not blocked by the compost washing down.

By using a standard compost the seeds are given a well-balanced diet and disease-free start to life. The John Innes composts have been used with success for many years, but good quality loam, an essential ingredient in their composition has become very hard to find.

For those people who prefer to mix their own compost the formula for the John Innes seed compost is: 2 parts sterilized loam, 1 part horticultural peat, 1 part lime-free coarse sand (all measured by volume).

To each bushel (four bucketfuls) of the mixture add 1½ oz. (40 g) superphosphate of lime and ¾ oz. (20 g) of chalk or ground limestone.

The potting compost is richer in plant foods. Seedlings are transferred into this from the seed compost when large enough to handle. Potting compost is composed of: 7 parts sterilized loam, 3 parts medium-grade peat, 2 parts lime-free coarse sand.

To each bushel of the mixture add 1½ oz. (40 g) hoof and horn (failing this one of the modern nitrogen substitutes), 1½ oz. (40 g) superphosphate, ¾ oz. (20 g) sulphate of potash, ¾ oz. (20 g) chalk or ground limestone.

John Innes base fertilizer is obtainable ready mixed as are the prepared composts.

The loam should be sterilized to a temperature of 180°F (82°C) to make sure no weed seeds or pests and diseases which could harm the plants are left alive. Sieve the loam through a ⅜ inch (1 cm) riddle. Use horticultural-grade moss peat. The sand must be coarse, lime-free and graded up to ⅜ inch (1 cm) particles.

On top of the drainage material in the pot place a thin layer of rough peat to stop the fine compost washing down to block the drainage hole. Place the prepared compost on top of this and firm gently so that the finished level comes about ½ inch (1½ cm) below the rim of the container. Use a pot press to firm the surface of the compost smooth and even.

With the good loam John Innes composts need becoming hard to find, composts based on peat have now been developed. Seed germinates and grows quickly in these but plants need feeding if they have to remain in them for any length of time. Peat-based composts in plastic pots tend to dry out more slowly in winter yet in hot sunny weather they dry out very quickly, so considerable care is required to ensure they are watered correctly.

Whatever compost is used, it must be thoroughly and evenly moist. Before you sow the seeds you must immerse the pots up to their rims in a bowl of water. Once the bubbles have stopped forming on the surface the whole pot is properly soaked.

Seed must be sown thinly as overcrowding causes weak growth and disease. Large seeds can be spaced out individually so that each has a fair share of space. This can save a lot of unnecessary work in pricking out. They are covered with compost to approximately their own depth. Fine seed like lobelia or begonia should be mixed with sand or crushed brick to make sure they are not overcrowded. The mixture is dusted thinly over the compost; then not covered but just firmed lightly with a pot press. This is the method used with African violets which germinate better in daylight.

Label each tray with the name of the seed, and to stop the compost drying out cover the pans with a pane of glass and newspaper.

A temperature of 55°F. (13°C) is essential for the seeds to germinate. A box over a radiator in the home, over the pipes in a greenhouse or fitted with electrically-heated soil-warming cables provides this warmth where it is most needed in the soil. Soil warming cables are easy to install. They are laid on 2 inches (5 cm) of sand, then covered with the same material. Pots plunged in peat up to their rims over soil-warming cables are kept at the correct temperature without drying out.

A propagator with a transparent cover of glass or plastic, fitted with a thermostatically-controlled heater which plugs into the mains system, may be purchased ready made-up. It provides equable conditions for germinating seeds or rooting cuttings, and is neat enough to use in the home without fear of damaging the furniture if used intelligently.

Once the seedlings have germinated and are large enough to handle they should be moved into a larger container before they become drawn, overcrowded or exhaust the available food in the seed mixture.

A standard seed tray made from wood or plastic measuring 8½ by 14 inches and 2½–3 inches deep (20 by 35 by 7 cm) makes the best container, unless the seedlings are to be transferred individually to small pots. Fill the tray with the potting compost then space the seedlings out in it 1–2 inches (3–5 cm) apart according to their size and the length of time they will be in the container. For growing them on, ideally, the greenhouse should be fitted with a staging. A 3 foot (90 cm) high bench about 40 inches wide (1 m) fitted with slats spaced ½–1 inch apart (1–2 cm) makes a good staging for plants to stand on, and is just the right height and width for watering.

All greenhouses should be fitted with adequate ventilation; they need at least two vents in the roof with others positioned as low as possible on the sides. This enables the gardener to regulate the fresh air supply so as to maintain good growing conditions. Greenhouses can be fitted with automatic openers which are governed by temperature, or electric extractor fans operated by a thermostat, but these refinements are expensive. Ventilators should be adjusted to keep a free movement of air without causing draughts.

Some shading is also required to protect tender-leaved plants during summer. Blinds made from wood, plastic or cotton are best as they can be adjusted according to the weather. Shading painted on the glass may be adequate but is a handicap if the weather turns dull.

Watering correctly is something which is learned by experience. No set of rules can be given but it is better to under- rather than over-water. How much and how often depends on the type of plant and the time of year. A plant in active growth under summer conditions may need watering twice a day, whereas for the same plant in winter once a month would be enough.

Where no greenhouse, frame or space in the house is available seed may be sown in pots then stood in a sheltered place outdoors. Seed such as cotoneaster, holly or primula will grow if sown into a sheltered nursery bed in the open garden. Germination will be slower and there is not the precise control over growing conditions which can be applied inside.

Cuttings and other propagating methods

Cuttings are described according to the stage of maturity at which they are taken.

softwood cutting semi-hardwood cutting hardwood cutting

Softwood cuttings

These cuttings, as the name implies, are made from the young growing tips of shrubs or, more often, greenhouse and herbaceous plants. Because both stems and leaves are immature they lose moisture quickly, so to achieve any sort of success they must be kept in warm humid conditions. A propagation frame, or a pot enclosed in a polythene bag are good methods of doing this.

Non-flowering shoots 2–4 inches (5–10 cm) long are cut with a sharp knife below the leaf joint. Cut away the bottom two leaves, dip the cut end in rooting powder, then insert the cutting close together in sharp lime-free sand. They must be kept well watered until it is obvious rooting has taken place and then potted up in a peat or soil based compost. Pure sand or 2 parts sand to 1 part peat make the most suitable rooting medium for all cuttings.

Semi-hardwood cuttings

These cuttings, 4–8 inches (10–20 cm) long, are made from shoots of the current season's wood which are just hardening at the base. Again a heated propagating bench or even a closed frame, unheated, help persuade the plants to root. Choose young healthy shoots cut either below a leaf node or with a sliver of wood (heel) from the main stem attached. Remove the lower leaves, dip the cut surface in rooting powder and insert in seed compost, then keep well watered until rooted. July to August is regarded as the semi-hardwood season.

Hardwood cuttings

These are the most fool-proof means of propagating the majority of shrubs commonly seen in gardens. Shoots which have grown the previous summer are cut either below a bud or with a heel of old wood. A length of 8–10 inches (20–25 cm) is suitable.

Make a narrow trench in a sheltered border, straight at the back and sloping at the front, 6–8 inches (15–20 cm) deep. Put a layer of coarse sand in the bottom and the cuttings are pushed into this after being treated with rooting powder. Replace the soil and firm well with a boot heel. Hardwood cuttings will take a year at least to root.

Root cuttings

Some plants, particularly those with thick fleshy roots may be propagated from sections of roots 2–3 inches (5–8 cm) long. Autumn is the best time for taking the root sections which are laid in seed trays filled with sandy compost and covered with the same material. Shoots appear the following spring and the young plants are ready for potting up.

Leaf cuttings

These are a useful method of raising large quantities of plants when the supply of rootable materials is limited. One African violet (Saintpaulia) will provide several leaves just approaching maturity which are suitable for rooting. The leaves are inserted upright in a sandy compost. Large leaves like the begonia are nicked with a razor blade across the larger veins. The leaf is then pegged down with the undersurface flat on the compost. In due course roots and young leaves develop at each cut. Leaves of shrubs such as the camellia taken with a section of stem and a bud will also root if inserted in a compost of 2 parts sand, 1 part peat.

Root division

Division of the root is possible with plants such as delphiniums. These plants produce several stems. When pulled away from the parent plant with sufficient roots attached, each stem is capable of growing into a separate individual.

Some shrubs have what are commonly termed suckers. A bud forms on the roots at some distance from the parent plant and grows into a strong shoot. Raspberries are an example. The root can be cut away with the shoot attached and planted up in a new bed if required.

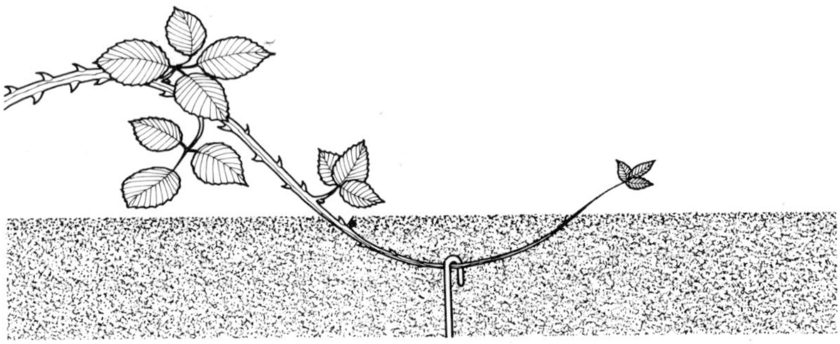

Layering

This is the easiest method of propagating climbing roses and clematis, because the cutting is persuaded to root while still attached to the parent. In the autumn choose conveniently-placed young shoots formed during the previous summer. Fork up the soil round the parent plant, bend the branch down, then make a hole in the ground where the stem touches about 12–15 inches (30–40 cm) from the tip is best. Fill the hole with a compost of 2 parts sand, 1 part peat. Either twist the branch to break *but not sever* the wood, or cut a tongue on the undersurface with a sharp knife. Push the wounded part of the branch into the compost, cover it. A large stone placed on the branch will hold it secure and keep the soil moist. Treating the wound with rooting powder makes roots grow quicker. Twelve to eighteen months later the rooted branch is severed from its parent and planted elsewhere in the garden.

Air layering

This is practised when the branch is too stiff for pulling down to soil level. Select a young shoot of one-year-old wood. With a sharp knife make a tongue $1\frac{1}{2}$ inches (4 cm) long, dust the cut surfaces with rooting powder, place a match stalk or piece of sphagnum between the two surfaces to hold them open. A piece of polythene is slipped over the branch to enclose the wound, packed full with sphagnum, then sealed at the top and bottom. Root development can be seen through the plastic and the young rooted branch severed and potted up.

Grafting

A piece of one plant (the scion) is united to the root of another plant (the rootstock) in such a way that they unite and become as one. Grafting is used when a shrub or tree does not easily root from cuttings. Line out young healthy stocks in well-prepared soil fifteen months prior to grafting. Keep them well watered and weed-free. Suitable scion material is collected during the dormant period (December to February) and tied up in bundles. To ensure the scion wood stays dormant plunge them in sand on the shady side of the house. 2 inches (5 cm) of sand round the base of the bundle is enough.

When the stocks start to grow in spring remove the top growth to the required height (usually 4–18 inches (10–45 cm) above soil level). A long slanting cut 1–2 inches (3–5 cm) long is made with a sharp bladed knife up the root stock. The knife is reversed to make a small slanting cut or tongue downwards across the face of the first cut. A similar matching cut is made in the scion and a tongue made to fit in the tongue on the stock. The two cut surfaces should fit flush together, with the *cambium layer* (the actively growing area immediately below the bark) firmly in contact with each other. Bind scion and stock together with raffia or a patent tie and make the join watertight with grafting wax. Water seeping down between the two can prevent a union. This method is known as *whip* and *tongue* grafting.

Grafting (whip and tongue)

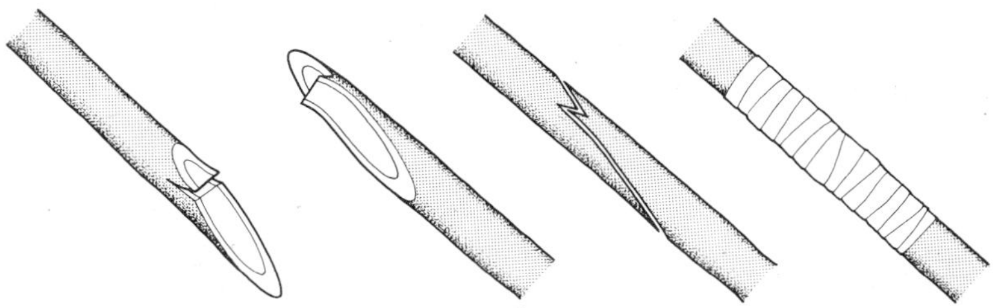

A *saddle graft* commonly used for rhododendron and softer-stemmed shrubs is equally simple to achieve. An inverted V or saddle cut is made in the stock and the scion is shaped to fit straddled over it. Both cuts are tied together, then sealed with grafting wax.

Budding

In the amateur field budding is largely confined to roses. The stocks are lined out in fertile, weed-free soil in late October to be budded the following summer when in full growth. For budding to be successful the bark should lift easily from the wood so the bud shield can be slipped in without damage. This condition occurs most frequently in showery, humid weather when there is also less danger of the bud drying out.

Scrape the soil away from the rootstock with a trowel as the bud needs to be placed at or below soil level. Wipe the point of budding with a damp cloth to clean it of soil. Choose plump firm buds which are usually found in the central section of shoots which have flowered. Make a cut across the rootstock, then another at right angles up to meet it and form a T. Remove the bud from the branch with a sharp knife starting the cut half an inch below the bud and the same

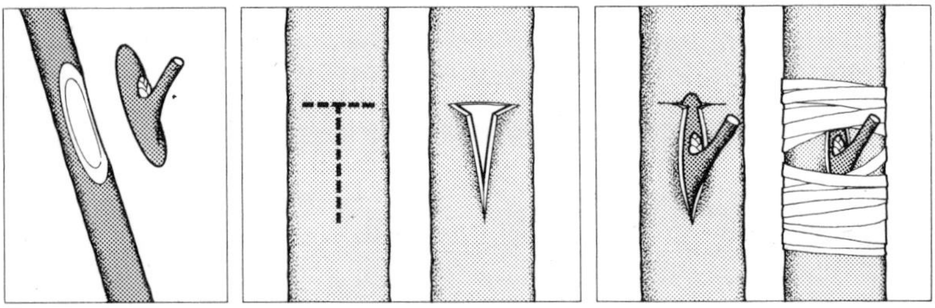

distance above. End with a twist of the wrist so the last piece of bark is torn away. Push the bud down between the two flaps made by the top of the T as far as it will go. The torn flap is trimmed flush with the top of the T and the wound made fast with raffia or a bud tie. Do not cover the bud. Trim the leaf but leave the stalk protruding as a marker to indicate when the bud has taken.

Standard roses and fruit trees are also budded in summer but the buds are inserted 4–6 feet ($1\frac{1}{4}$–$1\frac{3}{4}$ m) above soil level. Briar rose stocks are allowed to grow three or four shoots at the required level; the buds are put into these. Rugosa rose stocks are budded direct onto the main stem, the budding process is the same as previously described.

Index